Intellectual Property in the Energy Sector

Challenges and Opportunities for an Industry in Transition

Editor
Jon Moorhouse

Managing director
Sian O'Neill

Intellectual Property in the Energy Sector: Challenges and Opportunities for an Industry in Transition
is published by

Globe Law and Business Ltd
3 Mylor Close
Horsell
Woking
Surrey GU21 4DD
United Kingdom
Tel: +44 20 3745 4770
www.globelawandbusiness.com

Printed and bound in Great Britain by Ashford Colour Press Ltd

Intellectual Property in the Energy Sector: Challenges and Opportunities for an Industry in Transition

ISBN 9781787428102
EPUB ISBN 9781787428119
Adobe PDF ISBN 9781787428126

Table of contents

Introduction

Jon Moorhouse
Keystone Law

The energy industry is going through a period of huge upheaval. With diverging perspectives and budgets between the different stakeholders worldwide at an individual, corporate and national level, the transition to cleaner and greener energy sources will be neither easy nor quick. This was starkly evidenced by the somewhat muted progress achieved at the UN Climate Change Conference (COP26) in Glasgow at the end of 2021. The transition is, however, under way.

Innovation and the development of technology are central to this shift, with strong branding supporting its commercialisation and uptake by businesses and consumers. Intellectual property (IP) rights, in turn, play a fundamental role in the protection and exploitation of these technologies and brands.

The move away from traditional 'upstream' oil and gas exploration and production will be gradual as we manage the world's energy mix. New projects continue to come online, and there are still many long-term projects that will continue for many years to come. These are huge and complex operations involving the sharing and development of technology, data and know-how between multiple partners and presenting significant challenges and opportunities for all the parties involved. At the end of the life cycle of these fields, they will need to be decommissioned – always a challenging project in itself.

'Downstream' of oil and gas production, the world still has a seemingly insatiable appetite for oil products: petrol and diesel fuels, lubricants and so on. Even as we shift to renewables and reduce our reliance on oil and gas fuels, demand for these other products is not going away any time soon: electric vehicles (EV) and wind turbines are complex machines that still require lubricants. The confidential composition of these products, and the proprietary processes used to manufacture them, are critical to enabling a party to successfully differentiate itself from the competition and are very carefully and strategically protected via IP rights, including patents and trade secrets.

Renewable energy constitutes an increasingly significant proportion of the world's energy sources, and supply chains are already very well developed in some cases. The technical operator of a site generating wind or solar power may not always develop its own equipment – such as turbines, or solar panels and racks – and, instead, may choose to source it from specialist manufacturers. Protection via warranties or indemnities against third-party claims of IP infringement, therefore, plays an important part of the contractual arrangements for procurement. The operator will certainly develop its own know-how and methodologies to optimise site selection and project implementation, and will need to be very careful what it shares with competitors or engineering and procurement contractors.

The energy transition is playing out against a broader backdrop of the digitalisation of society and industry and the continued development of artificial intelligence (AI). Advances in these areas are helping to significantly improve efficiencies and safety across all aspects of the energy industry, from subsurface oil and gas exploration and production, to managing energy distribution and enabling predictive modelling in plants and operations. This brings with it fresh IP challenges and opportunities in terms of protection and exploitation of digital, software-based technology and 'big data'. Indeed, as well as the patentability of inventions relating to AI software, patent offices in different countries are now wrestling with the notion of inventorship by AI itself.

Whatever the source of the energy, whether hydrocarbon or electron based, the Internet of Things (IoT) is making its presence felt in the way energy is both distributed and consumed. The wireless interaction of all our household appliances, and of our cars with petrol or recharging forecourts, brings the energy industry into the realm of 'standard essential patents' (SEPs) and discussions as to what constitutes fair, reasonable and non-discriminatory (FRAND) licensing. Disputes as to who should pay a licence fee in relation to these patents, on what terms and at what level of the supply chain, are no longer solely the preserve of the telecoms industry and have the potential to impact materially on all of us.

Whatever area of the energy industry a business operates in, strong branding and reputation management are critical. Traditional oil and gas majors have global brands that have always been carefully managed to serve as indicators of reliability and safety in the face of unregulated counterfeit goods. As these companies now look to reposition themselves and improve their 'green' credentials, they face competition from smaller, disruptive 'new energy' start-ups who will be alert to the power of branding in an effort to boost their market share. Protection and exploitation of trademarks, design rights and copyright can exert a huge amount of influence on the business and consumer perception of these companies.

This Special Report takes a look at all of these areas, providing insight from the expert contributors of each of the chapters and, in some cases, from people working in the industry who kindly agreed to be interviewed. My thanks to all of the contributors and to Globe Law and Business for making this publication happen.

I hope you find this Special Report to be helpful food for thought in a fascinating area at a fascinating time. If you have any questions on anything you read, we would be happy to discuss this with you.

"Oil and gas exploration and production ('upstream') energy operations often take place on a huge scale with very long life cycles and collaboration with a number of partners is the norm."

I. Energy joint ventures: upstream

Jon Moorhouse
Keystone Law

Oil and gas exploration and production ('upstream') energy operations often take place on a huge scale with very long life cycles and collaboration with a number of partners is the norm. In this chapter, we will look at sharing and creating technology and data and trade secrets on oil and gas field projects – from first exploration through to end of field life – and how energy companies can manage this process effectively to meet their business objectives.

For a project to succeed, several parties may need to contribute – or acquire or develop – critical information or technology. In the early stages of a project, this could take the form of either: (1) raw data concerning the identified field, rig or pipeline; or (2) interpretations of this data to understand the subsurface, operational performance or any safety concerns. It could be the sensors needed to acquire the raw data or the software or algorithms used to process and interpret this data. It usually involves collaboration between experienced personnel, with a lot of specialist know-how, and can mean the use of patented inventions or perhaps the use of valuable trade secrets.

The opportunities are substantial and, inevitably, so are the risks. It can be difficult to decide when and where to share or generate valuable and confidential data, know-how or trade secrets to execute the project successfully, whilst preventing it from leaking to competitors or to others who could use the information or replicate the technology themselves, so that they would have no need to come to you for the next project.

Conversely, how to ensure that the confidential data or information you are exposed to during the course of the project – shared by a project partner with you in confidence – does not 'contaminate' your own confidential data sets, know-how, research results and so on, potentially preventing you from independently exploiting, patenting or publishing your own results until your confidentiality obligations to your partner have ended?

In practice, this comes down to a combination of measures: carefully constructed contractual provisions concerning confidentiality and intellectual property (IP) ownership and use rights, along with the development – and well-managed implementation – of appropriate IP and information management governance processes.

Key collaborators in a traditional upstream project typically include the state owning the relevant oil or gas field, one or more energy companies contributing funding and possibly technology to the project, one party acting as an operator, and various contractor service companies. From the initial exploration for hydrocarbon reserves through to the plugging, abandonment and decommissioning of a well, it is not uncommon for the whole process to take over 30 years, with different technologies involved at each stage.

1. Exploration

Techniques for finding oil and gas reserves and correctly identifying where to drill are increasingly sophisticated and, increasingly, digitised and data-driven.

1.1 Data acquisition

If the geophysical data for a proposed field is not already available, it will need to be acquired in order to assess the prospects of successfully finding and extracting the hydrocarbons located there.

The notion of a source sending a signal subsurface and a receiver to capture whatever is bounced back is not new and hence not patentable *per se*. Nor is the use of micro-electromechanical systems to create tiny integrated devices made using integrated circuit batch processing techniques (eg, sensors to capture the data, in a geophone in a land-based seismic survey).

However, there may be valuable – and potentially patentable – IP in the fabrication techniques and, more specifically for the energy industry, in exactly what signals are used and what waves are then recorded in different environments to generate the most accurate understanding of the relevant subsurface.

Offshore, the use of pressure-sensitive transducers in hydrophone receivers in marine seismic acquisition is, again, not new. However, the particular signals generated and 'sweeps' carried out towing arrays of sensors for optimal acquisition in any given area may well constitute valuable know-how or trade secrets, or even patentable inventions (see the 'Marine seismic acquisition' box below).

Marine seismic acquisition

Upstream-related patents have been sought and exploited strategically in large numbers in the energy industry, whether to carve out an exclusive position or perhaps to cross-license, or simply to secure 'bragging rights' to improve the chance of winning a tender for a new field. The energy industry is generally not very litigious. However, these patents do occasionally have their moment in court.

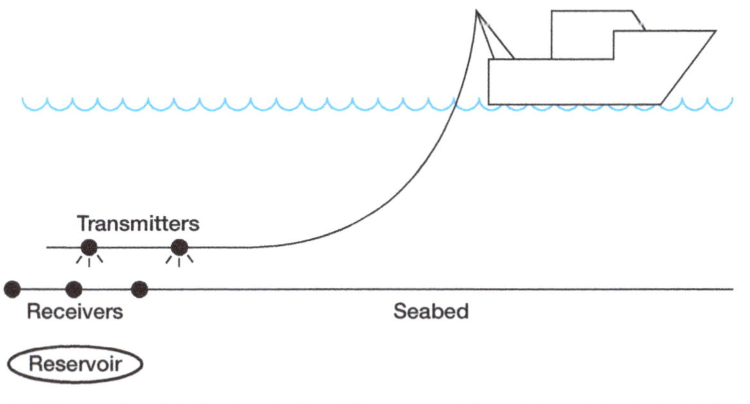

Method and apparatus for determining the nature of subterranean reservoirs (eg, European Patent (UK) No 1,256,019)

This patent held by Electromagnetic Geoservices AS related to the use of controlled source electromagnetism: measurements taken by towing transmitters over receivers placed on the seabed can be used to generate an idea of any underlying hydrocarbon reservoir.

The global service company Schlumberger considered this patent to be sufficiently important to merit challenging its validity in the English court in 2009. They won, but the decision was overturned on appeal. (See Schlumberger Holdings Ltd v Electromagnetic Geoservices AS [2010] EWCA Civ 819.)

The patentee, ElectroMagnetic GeoServices ASA, later brought an infringement action against a competitor PGS. There was a long trial but the case settled before judgment.

Increasingly, the sensor technology itself has been the subject of development, to the point where it has the capability to not only capture, but also store and even process data, before relaying to a central terminal.

It is an expensive exercise to capture fresh data on the scales and with the accuracy needed.

If already acquired, the seismic acquisition service providers may offer a 'multi-client' licence to more than one party to use the data. If a fresh survey is required, the parties will need to agree whether the exploration company will have an exclusive licence to use the data and, if so, at what additional cost, for what period of time, and so on.

Governments may already have data relating to relevant fields in their territory, and the national (state) oil companies may be prepared to enter into a data licence agreement with interested international oil companies, or perhaps a data exchange agreement (where, in return, the licensee of the raw data may share any resulting interpretations of the data).

Large data sets can be very valuable. (See the 'Protecting and commercialising data' box opposite.)

1.2 Data processing and interpretation

These data acquisition activities involve generating or sharing a huge amount of raw seismic data that needs to be processed and interpreted to generate a meaningful understanding of the subsurface in the field in question and, ultimately, of what reserves of oil and gas may be present.

Interpretative techniques usually involve complex algorithms and workflows, very often captured in software. (See Chapter IV to learn more about the protection of software.) The ability to provide accurate, reliable interpretations and projections of oil and gas production is a key differentiator guiding selection of one company over another for a project, and this IP is protected very carefully.

Different energy companies have taken different approaches to this. Some have sought to protect this capability via trade secrets, others by building up dense patent thickets to carve out an exclusive area. A company may be prepared to share the findings of applying its techniques to a set of raw data – the resulting interpretation – but never the techniques used.

This is often a factor in negotiating an early stage 'Joint Study Agreement' between perhaps a government owning a field and one or more industrial partners (oil and gas majors collaborating together,

"The ability to provide accurate, reliable interpretations and projections of oil and gas production is a key differentiator guiding selection of one company over another for a project, and this IP is protected very carefully."

say, and perhaps working with one of the oil and gas service companies). Even when collaborating, the actual interpretation of raw geophysical data may well be carried out 'in-house' using proprietary techniques rather than a truly collaborative effort. The collaboration may then come in to play around how to optimise production of the oil and gas identified, depending on what technical/geographical challenges and opportunities are identified.

Protecting and commercialising data

The protection and commercialisation of data itself, rather than related technology, is another key area. Should large data sets be made freely available to all, in line with the National Data Repository of the North Sea Transition Authority (until recently known as the UK Oil and Gas Authority)? This information can be very costly to generate and potentially extremely valuable.

In many jurisdictions, there is no property right to information or data *per se*, and parties have to rely on confidentiality rights or contractual rights.

However, in some countries, for example, in the Middle East, there may be legislation stipulating that the state owns all geophysical data relating to its territory, irrespective of who generates it. The most another party could aim to achieve would be a licence to use it. Even if the data set would be useful to develop interpretative techniques that could be applied in other parts of the world (eg, with similar formations), there is no guarantee the relevant state will grant this broader right: one of many bargaining chips.

Confidentiality rights and copyright can help to protect data. Database rights may also offer protection for large systematically ordered databases where there has been substantial investment in obtaining, verifying and presenting the data.

Many issues remain open, however. For example, in the case of machine learning: if a system is 'trained' on a valuable data set, who should benefit most from the resulting improved version – the owner of the original software or the provider of the data? This can be a key factor in the commercial negotiations concerning the use and licensing of software and functionality developed by use of huge data sets, even if the value is no longer in understanding what reservoirs of oil and gas may exist in any one particular field.

Key considerations for an organisation looking to protect and commercialise data include the following:

- Understand and be able to track the exact and full extent of the data in question.
- For geophysical data, clarify any local legislative constraints on ownership and use of that data for the relevant territory.
- Where appropriate, mark data sets as 'confidential' or 'proprietary' and include © markings on all related documents or software.
- Implement internal processes and working practices with partners to ensure confidentiality and use rights restrictions are maintained for your data and for any data you receive.

2. Production

Assuming the exploration went well, and interpretation and analysis of the data is promising, the project will proceed to 'production' of oil and gas from the field: setting up and 'completing' the wells created.

The drilling technology involved is complex and well protected (often via patents), always seeking to optimise flow of oil and gas to the surface in a controlled, safe way. Service companies are often engaged by the oil and gas company to carry out a lot of the tasks involved.

These are large operations with lots of equipment – and personnel – to manage. As well as the technology, the companies involved all have a wealth of operational know-how, with experienced professionals that again often distinguish one company over another for selection for a particular project. The parties need to find a way to cooperate yet still preserve the secrecy of their respective know-how and trade secrets. This can be significant when project lifetimes can outlast the life of a patent, and so it may be preferable to protect some technology as a trade secret with no fixed end-date, rather than via a patent which would ultimately leave the original invention in the public domain and free for others to use after approximately 20 years.

In Europe at least, there has been increased harmonisation of the protection of trade secrets following the Trade Secrets Directive 2016,[1] including alignment on a definition of what constitutes a trade secret. In essence:

- information/ideas that are not generally available to the public;
- that are commercially valuable to those that have the information/idea because it is not known to others (and so offers a competitive advantage); and
- in relation to which appropriate steps are taken to keep the information/ideas confidential.

This latter requirement means energy companies need to be able to demonstrate that they have some form of trade secret capture programme, to separately and securely record and store this information with controlled access rights. The directive did not change the landscape much in the UK when it was an EU member state and, post-Brexit, the UK's well-developed laws of confidentiality continue to support the protection of trade secrets and, indeed, other confidential information or know-how. The position is also similar in the US following the introduction of the Defend Trade Secrets Act. (See Chapter IV for more on the US position.)

All of this comes into play when putting in place the necessary project arrangements – contractual and operational governance. Governance is discussed later in this chapter. First, we will take a look at the contractual arrangements.

Typically, there will be a 'production sharing agreement' or 'concession agreement' with the government, as well as an agreement between venture partners. As between the venture partners – that is, the energy companies funding the operation and who will benefit from a proportion of the oil or gas produced – there will be a joint venture arrangement. This could involve setting up an incorporated joint venture entity in which the partners take a shareholding. However, very often upstream joint ventures do not involve an incorporated entity and the parties will enter into a Joint Operating Agreement (JOA) that, amongst other things, governs exactly what each party

"The definition of 'Joint Property' could be construed to include IP, which the operator may want to avoid."

will contribute in terms of funding, personnel and technology, and what rights each party will have. There are various industry bodies offering standard agreements that the parties can use, at least as a starting point. These include the Logic agreements often used for UK oil and gas operations, and the suite of template agreements developed by the Association of International Petroleum Negotiators (AIPN). (See the 'Model joint operating agreements' box below for more on model JOAs.)

These projects also usually involve the secondment of significant numbers of personnel. Secondments are often handled via separate agreements which need to be clear on what information or other IP the secondees will share, and on what basis.

Model joint operating agreements

These agreements have to cover a very large range of complex operational and financial issues, and the parties need to be careful when working with the standard definitions and clauses to ensure that technology, data and know-how, and associated ownership and use rights, are handled appropriately, where they are captured within broader contractual references to 'property' intended to cover tangible property as well.

For example, the AIPN model JOA, uses broad definitions of 'Joint Property' and 'Venture Information'.

The definition of 'Joint Property' could be construed to include IP, which the operator may want to avoid.

If any technology is developed whilst operating the field, it is likely to be a development of the operator's own technology.

If this was developed with joint funding from all participants (ie, not just the operator), should they all co-own this improvement, or should the operator own it and perhaps offer some rights of use back to the other participants instead? Should the operator offer a licence to its underlying 'background' IP as well?

The definition of 'Venture Information' is most likely intended to cover geophysical and drilling data, and by default is deemed to be Joint Property, where each party is entitled to receive and use Venture Information. However, in reality it could also be construed to include improvements or developments of one or more parties' technology.

Should Venture Information include any information or data, or IP or technology, acquired or generated by a party (eg, the operator) at its own expense, or should it be restricted just to what is created using joint project funding?

In practice, although model agreements are a great starting point, the drivers and business objectives for each participant will vary for each individual field, and the parties will need to think carefully about the above issues and be prepared to seek to adapt any model to meet their specific requirements.

Energy companies, therefore, need to think through these provisions very carefully before the start of a project, with a good understanding of short- and long-term business objectives, and of the company's supporting short- and long-term IP strategy for the relevant technologies involved. Further considerations include:

- Will the energy company be the operator, using and contributing its own technology on the project?
- For any technology or data it wishes to contribute to the project, is it comfortable with the IP protection it has in place for this before sharing? For example, for trade secrets: as well as the confidentiality provisions of the project agreement, have appropriate measures been taken to identify and separately store and manage the trade secrets?

- Over the potentially long lifetime of a project, how it will keep track of what information or other IP it will share and receive?
- What risk assessment processes does it have in place before, for example, agreeing to receive trade secrets, know-how or other confidential data from project partners on a confidential basis? (See the 'Managing confidential information – leakage and contamination' box opposite.)
- To what extent should affiliates of each of the project partners receive the right to use IP developed in the project, and any relevant 'background' IP of the other parties?
- To what extent should these use rights extend to use on other projects, perhaps where the IP owner is not involved? For what time period and in which territories?
- What technology is actually needed for successful implementation of the project? Does the production sharing agreement or JOA require the energy company to use its most advanced technology and to share it with the relevant state oil company and/or the other parties (and perhaps even provide 'tech transfer' services to show them how to use it)? If so, what risk does this pose for those other companies to be enabled to work on further fields without needing to involve that energy company next time?

"On receiving information from a third party in confidence, there is a risk that this information could become mixed up with – or 'contaminate' – the energy company's own research results, know-how or other data."

- Should any use rights granted continue even for a party after it leaves the venture? (Does the relevant government have the right to remove the energy company from the project after a number of years but perhaps with a continued licence to the company's technology?)
- What access controls will be imposed for secondees from other participants who wish to see and use the energy company's information and technology? Would they have access to proprietary systems, perhaps even trade secrets?

An energy company may look to provide services itself, using its own proprietary technology, and simply share the results with its partners, rather than granting a licence to use its technology.

Managing confidential information – leakage and contamination

Leakage

What is the risk for an energy company of its confidential technology/information/know-how leaking to its project partners, so that they are able to use it elsewhere perhaps without needing to engage the energy company, or even proceeding to further develop and patent an improved version that the energy company cannot use without a licence?

The energy company will need to include appropriate confidentiality and restricted use provisions in the relevant project agreements AND even with those provisions are in place, consider whether they should still share certain information and trade secrets, or perhaps simply provide the service using the technology themselves and simply share the results (eg, interpretation of raw seismic data).

Contamination

On receiving information from a third party in confidence, there is a risk that this information could become mixed up with – or 'contaminate' – the energy company's own research results, know-how or other data. In order to comply with the confidentiality and restricted use obligations imposed by the project agreement, it has to keep the whole lot secret, which may significantly impact on its plans to patent, otherwise publish or exploit its own data and information. It can happen that individuals and whole teams are contaminated and need to be ring-fenced for a period of time after working on a project.

This can be managed by being careful what information the energy company agrees to share and receive in confidence: agreeing upfront with the other parties what can be shared and with whom. Personnel need to be well trained to be alert to this, to mark relevant materials they share (in hard/soft copy) 'confidential' (or perhaps 'most confidential' or another more stringent marking if the company agrees it is appropriate to share highly prized trade secrets), and to follow up with written confirmation of things shared orally in meetings.

Staff should be encouraged to step out of meetings if confidential information is to be shared that it does not want to receive, and record that they have done so.

3. End of field life

When a well is depleted to the extent that it is no longer economically viable to extract further hydrocarbons, the final phase may be to 'plug' it safely before abandoning it, and perhaps removing in whole or part the rigs involved. The decommissioning of a field at the end of its life cycle in a safe and environmentally friendly way can throw up further technical challenges, with a further collaborative project phase entailing a lot of the same considerations as described above. There is a common concern between all parties to ensure this is done with personal and environmental safety in mind, and there may a strong case for sharing know-how. However, this know-how – including, for example, reliable methods to assess the likely costs of a decommissioning project – can be valuable in itself.

Another possibility is the repurposing of empty or depleted reservoirs for the storage of captured CO_2. Carbon capture and storage is one route to reduced emissions and the above considerations again apply to the development and implementation of technology for capturing this technology and then ensuring safe storage underground.

4. Intellectual property management

A large energy company may well have different departments or business units leading decision making on different aspects of IP. For example, the R&D department may lead on creating IP strategies for different technologies and hence decisions on whether, and how, to protect particular inventions. However, in the context of large collaborative projects, it may be a different commercial or business development team that negotiates the project arrangements and hence agrees to commitments on the acquisition, development and licensing of relevant data, information and technology.

It may well be a separate marketing team that drives the company's brand strategy that, in turn, then guides decisions in the protection and exploitation of trademarks. (See Chapter VI on brand protection for more on this.)

Internal governance is essential to ensure that the application of technology across the company (or group of companies) is consistently aligned with the relevant IP strategy. For example, if the R&D department decides to protect an algorithm for seismic data interpretation as a trade secret, not to be shared with anyone outside the company, this is no good if the commercial team negotiating the terms of the JOA agrees to share with venture partners, even if under confidentiality arrangements. The idea could leak and destroy the company's competitive advantage.

This governance needs to be implemented by all energy company personnel. Decisions may be made by team leaders, but the whole team must then be required to act in line with that decision. The energy company can look to develop standards and policies that its staff must comply with – including in relation to IP, on protecting the company's IP assets and being careful not to infringe the IP rights of others. (See Chapter II for more on freedom of action studies and dealing with third-party IP rights.)

Processes can be put in place, for example, on information management, which staff can follow. For example, if they wish to share information with a project partner, ideally there would be an internal approval process, with sign-off perhaps from the team lead and, if

"The energy company can look to develop standards and policies that its staff must comply with – including in relation to IP, on protecting the company's IP assets and being careful not to infringe the IP rights of others."

different, someone with appropriate authority from the R&D team as well. Compliance with IP standards and protocols can perhaps be included in staff contracts with the potential for disciplinary action for non-compliance to ensure this is given sufficient attention. Further, onboarding and offboarding of personnel should be managed carefully, to ensure they do not share with their new employer information from their previous employer which continues to be the subject of secrecy and restricted use obligations. Exit interviews can be used to remind a departing employee that they must still keep relevant information confidential even after they leave, and perhaps also to ensure valuable know-how is captured for the company from experienced employees before they go.

Where the energy company then works with others on a large project, ideally further governance processes, standards and policies should be put in place for the joint venture itself. For an incorporated joint venture vehicle, this may be a case of the parties agreeing what standards the joint venture company should adopt. For unincorporated joint ventures, governance may be via protocols, fleshing out key principles on IP and confidentiality that are captured in the JOA.

This can be bolstered by ensuring staff receive adequate IP training, to help ensure they understand the IP risks and are clear on the consequences – for themselves as individuals as well as for the business – if they do not comply with the company's IP rules.

Technology may also help with IP management, for example, information access controls for employees seconded from project partners or software that alerts you when large amounts of data are transferred outside of your organisation.

Notes

1 Directive (EU) 2016/943 of the European Parliament and of the Council of 8 June 2016 on the protection of undisclosed know-how and business information (trade secrets) against their unlawful acquisition, use and disclosure, https://eur-lex.europa.eu/legal-content/EN/TXT/?uri=CELEX%3A32016L0943.

II. A downstream perspective

Maeve O'Flynn
Finnegan Europe LLP
Paul Townsend
Finnegan LLP

Many energy businesses combine their upstream activities with a range of downstream activities in which oil and gas are refined, processed and transformed into a range of products. Many renewables businesses produce similar products from alternative feedstocks. This chapter addresses the intellectual property (IP) opportunities and risks that are encountered when operating within downstream technology areas.

Downstream innovation can be broadly categorised into: (1) technology relating primarily to process innovation; and (2) technology relating to differentiated products. We address the challenges arising from protecting and monetising technology in both these areas.

1. Process technology

Downstream technology may be directed to the preparation of a commodity product, such as a petrochemical feedstock or a fuel. These products may not be innovative: they may even be identical to competitor products. However, the processes that make these products are often highly innovative and enterprises that develop these processes will seek to protect and monetise their process innovation.

1.1 How can process technology be protected?

Process technology can be protected as a trade secret. This is applicable where the process technology embodies information that is not known to the public, and the owner of the technology makes reasonable efforts to maintain the secrecy of the information.

Trade secret protection is likely to be appropriate for valuable process information such as: (1) preferred operating conditions; (2) start-up and shut-down protocols; (3) methods of checking and maintaining quality; and (4) reactor set-up. However, the challenges of maintaining confidentiality and the potential risk of losing freedom to operate should not be underestimated. The opportunities and challenges of trade secret protection are addressed in Chapter I of this Special Report.

For many process innovations, patent protection may be the preferred tool for preventing competitors from using or offering the same, or similar, technology. Patents can protect process innovations, but owners of process patents face challenges that are not typically encountered with patents for products.

1.2 What protection is offered by process patents?

Article 28 1(b) of the TRIPS Agreement states that, where the subject matter of a patent is a process:

> 1. *A patent shall confer on its owner the following exclusive rights:*
>
> *(b) where the subject matter of a patent is a process, to prevent third parties not having the owner's consent from the act of using the process, and from the acts of: using, offering for sale, selling, or importing for these purposes at least the product obtained directly by that process.*[1]

A process patent can, therefore, exclude competitors from using a process and from marketing the products resulting from such a process. However, the protection offered by a process patent will only be commercially useful if the process has been appropriately captured in the patent. The enforceable scope of a patent is defined by the claims of the patent. A process claim will typically consist of several different process steps. For example, a process for making product X could include the following steps:

(1) heating feedstock A in the presence of catalyst B to provide intermediate C;
(2) adding solvent D to intermediate C to provide mixture E; and
(3) separating mixture E by filtration to provide product X.

"Process technology can be protected as a trade secret. This is applicable where the process technology embodies information that is not known to the public, and the owner of the technology makes reasonable efforts to maintain the secrecy of the information."

In order to infringe this claim, the competitor must either use all the steps of the process (steps (1), (2) and (3)) or the competitor must market product X obtained directly by the claimed process.

1.3 In which circumstances will competitor activity be outside the scope of protection of your process patent?

(a) Scenario 1: Is a competitor carrying out all the steps of the process?
Problems can arise if a competitor is carrying out some, but not all, of the steps in the process. With the claim above, a competitor might find that intermediate C is commercially available. The competitor can purchase intermediate C and then carry out steps (2) and (3) to obtain product X. Alternatively, two competitors could work together to make product X, with competitor 1 carrying out steps (1) and (2) in its plant, then shipping mixture E to the plant of competitor 2 in a neighbouring country, where step (3) is carried out. In both of these scenarios, because there is no single party carrying out all the claimed steps in a single territory, it will be difficult to establish infringement of the process patent.

Most jurisdictions have a concept of 'joint infringement' or 'divided infringement' that addresses the scenario where different process steps are carried out by different parties within the same territory, but this is typically complex. For example, Korean courts will consider whether there are multiple actors who are each aware of the other actors' partial implementation of the patented invention, and who intend to make use of the actors' partial implementation of the patent.

Nalco Co v Chem-Mod LLC[2] addressed the issue of divided infringement in the US. The patent involved a process for treating coal combustion flue gas containing mercury. The plaintiffs alleged that certain defendants made coal using a 'Chem-Mod Solution' that contained additives for treating the combusted coal, and then controlled or directed infringement of the claims at issue through the testing of the 'Chem-Mod Solution' on pilot scale and full scale at the University of North Dakota and at coal-fired power plants. The court held that divided infringement could apply here. Divided infringement applies where "an entity would be held responsible for the performance of method steps by others where that entity directs or controls others' performance, or where the actors formed a joint enterprise".[3] The court further noted that divided infringement applies where "an alleged infringer conditions participation in an activity or receipt of a benefit upon performance of a step or steps of a patented method and established the manner and timing of that performance".[4] The court held that the plaintiffs sufficiently pled infringement of

"Most jurisdictions have a concept of 'joint infringement' or 'divided infringement' that addresses the scenario where different process steps are carried out by different parties within the same territory, but this is typically complex."

claims at issue at either the University of North Dakota or various coal-fired power plants, and the plaintiffs sufficiently pled that the performance of the testing was attributed to the actions of the defendants because the performance was conditioned on obtaining monetary benefits from the defendants.

In *Travel Sentry Inc v Tropp*,[5] the US patent involved a method of improving airline inspection by an airline inspection entity. The defendant met the first two steps of the method claim at issue simply by manufacturing and selling a special lock for airline luggage, but at issue was whether the final two steps – carried out by the Transportation Security Administration (TSA) – could be attributable to the defendant. In evaluating whether the defendant was liable for direct infringement due to the TSA's actions, the court noted that a common thread in divided-infringement cases was whether there was "evidence that a third party hoping to obtain access to certain benefits can only do so if it performs certain steps identified by the defendant, and does so under the terms prescribed by the defendant".[6] The court held that a memorandum of understanding (MOU) signed between the defendant and the TSA indicated that the "TSA believed it would receive some benefit from the arrangement"[7] and that the benefit was conditioned on the TSA carrying out the final two steps of the claim at issue. Next, the court held that the MOU established the manner or timing of the TSA's performance because the "MOU sets forth the steps TSA would need to follow in order to use [defendant's] standard and obtain the associated benefits".[8] Finally, the court noted that the "context of this case can justify attributing TSA's performance"[9] to the defendants because the defendant had the right and ability to stop or limit the TSA's ability to practise the final two steps of the claims through various means.

Where the different steps are carried out in different territories, establishing infringement becomes even more difficult. There are some circumstances under which courts have found infringement even when one process step has been carried out in a different territory, but such cases typically relate to computer-implemented inventions where the steps are carried out on servers located in different countries. With downstream process technology, it will be very difficult to establish infringement when a claimed process is carried out across multiple territories.

(b) Scenario 2: Is a competitor marketing a product obtained directly by the claimed process?

Problems can also arise if a competitor is marketing a product derived from product X in the claim discussed above. The critical question for infringement is whether the marketed article is the direct product of the claimed process?

Product X is clearly the direct product of the patented process. However, if product X is materially changed (eg, by reaction with another chemical entity) or is incorporated as a minor component in a formulation (eg, by addition at ppm levels to another product), then it will be difficult to establish that there is infringement of the process claim.

The UK courts established a test for the 'direct product' in *Pioneer Electronics Capital Inc v Warner Music Manufacturing GmbH*.[10] The court considered that a product could be a direct product even if further processing had occurred. The critical question was whether there was a loss of identity. There would be no loss of identity if the product retained its essential characteristics. This reasoning was followed in *Medimmune Ltd v Novartis Pharmaceuticals UK Ltd*,[11] relating to biotechnological methods. The invention was, arguably, in the early steps of the claimed process. However, the court upheld the identity test; it was not relevant for the purposes of infringement that the later steps in the claimed process were conventional manufacturing steps.

In the US, US Code Title 35[12] states that a product that is made by a patented process will not be considered an infringing product if it is materially changed by subsequent processes, or it becomes a trivial and non-essential component of another product.

In *Syngenta Crop Protection LLC v Willowood LLC*,[13] certain claims were directed to a group of chemical compounds, including azoxystrobin – a fungicide commonly used in agriculture to control fungal growth on crops – and directed towards a chemical process for manufacturing azoxystrobin. The district court determined that the azoxystrobin at issue was manufactured in China using the patented process. However, the district court stated that one party is required to conduct every step of the process for §271(g) to apply. At trial, the jury determined that the process was not conducted completely by one party, and thus §271(g) could not apply to the azoxystrobin sold in the US. The Federal Circuit disagreed, holding that "under §271(g), whether [a] process is practiced by a single entity is immaterial to the infringement analysis under that section".[14] In particular, the court noted that "the focus [of the statutory language] is only on acts with respect to *products* resulting from the patented process".[15] No liability actually arises from practising the process. Accordingly, the court remanded the case to the district court for further proceedings.

1.4 How do you ensure that the claims of your process patent provide commercially useful protection?

A process patent will only provide effective protection for your commercial process – and the products thereof – if you have appropriately captured the process in the claims of your patent. Questions that must be considered when drafting and prosecuting the patent application include:

- Does the claim have too many steps such that one or more steps are likely to be carried out by another party or even in another territory? For example, is it possible that an intermediate could become commercially available during the lifetime of the patent?
- Does the claim have too few steps such that the product that will be marketed by competitors is not the direct product of the patented process? For example, if your product is going to be incorporated into a fuel, have you included a process claim for making a fuel? If your product is a feedstock for polymer manufacture, have you included process claims for making the polymer and for making polymeric articles from the polymer?
- Are there alternative ways of claiming your process innovation? For example, is it possible to draft a claim to an apparatus corresponding to your innovative reactor design or is it possible to claim the catalyst used in your innovative catalytic process?

"A process patent will only provide effective protection for your commercial process – and the products thereof – if you have appropriately captured the process in the claims of your patent."

A commercial outlook during the entire patenting process, from initial drafting all the way through to grant, is needed in order to obtain protection that is commercially meaningful.

1.5 Will you be able to prove infringement of your process patent?

Even if the scope of your process claims is appropriate, you may still encounter difficulties enforcing the claims because it can be difficult to obtain evidence that definitively establishes that your competitor is carrying out the process or is marketing a product obtained directly from that process.

This can be particularly difficult in legal jurisdictions where discovery is not available for gathering evidence. However, this problem has been recognised by some countries and there have been legislative amendments to allow for a shift in the burden of proof. In both China and Korea, the defendant cannot simply deny infringement of the process patent but must provide evidence that they do not infringe. In Japan, a new inspection system has recently become available, allowing the patentee to request a court-ordered inspection, in which a court-designated inspector visits a site of the alleged infringer to collect necessary evidence.

Even in the US, where discovery is available to obtain evidence, and in Europe, where the enforcement directive enables the gathering and preservation of evidence, it may still be difficult, and potentially costly, to gather evidence establishing infringement of process patents. When considering how to protect your downstream process innovation, particularly with respect to geographical scope of patent protection, the potential difficulties of proving infringement should be considered.

1.6 What is the value of your process patents?

Given all the challenges outlined above, what is the true value of process patents for your downstream technology? If you get your claims right (not too many or too few process steps) and ensure that you choose the right territories (where your competitors have plants and where they are selling) then it is possible to have enforceable rights that will enable you to exclude competitors from operating the claimed process technology or selling products resulting from that process.

Process patents can be especially valuable if you plan to monetise your process innovation by licensing the technology to third parties. Process patents, even of narrow scope, can be an indication to your potential licensees that the technology is innovative, exclusive and, therefore, valuable. The licensee's primary concern might be access to technical know-how, but a considered and comprehensive schedule of

"When considering how to protect your downstream process innovation, particularly with respect to geographical scope of patent protection, the potential difficulties of proving infringement should be considered."

patent rights, in the relevant territories, can be an important part of the licence offer.

Process patents are also valuable in cross-licensing scenarios when one party seeks access to another party's technology. A portfolio of technologically relevant process patents can provide significant leverage during the negotiation of a cross-licence.

A strategy of pursuing process patents can be valuable even in the scenario when none of the patent applications ever results in granted, enforceable rights. Patent applications are published 18 months after the filing date, or priority date if priority is claimed, and such publications can be immensely valuable when establishing freedom to operate in view of competitors' process patents. Of course, any publication could serve this purpose (eg, disclosures at conferences or in academic journals) but the detail and rigour required in a patent application can mean that this type of publication is more effective in establishing freedom to operate as compared to other types of disclosure.

Process patents, despite the many challenges in crafting and enforcing such patents, are a valuable commercial tool for any developer of innovative downstream technology.

"Innovators of differentiated products in the downstream space will seek to protect and monetise their innovation. They will also need to ensure that they have freedom to operate for all the products in their extensive product portfolios."

2. Differentiated products

Products made from oil and gas are not always commodities, in fact, many are highly differentiated. Products derived from renewable feedstocks may provide similar or improved performance compared to those derived from oil and gas, and can also offer sustainability benefits.

Differentiated gasoline and diesel are available on many forecourts and command higher prices from consumers eager to maximise the performance and/or efficiency of their vehicle. Even with the imminent shift to electric vehicles (EV), it will be some time before conventionally fuelled vehicles disappear. Electric vehicles will not require liquid fuels, but a variety of lubricants – derived from oil and gas or renewable feedstocks – will continue to play a vital role in transportation.

Specialised lubricants are also used in a vast array of non-transport applications. Lubricants play an important role in renewable energy technology such as wind turbines and can offer significant improvements in performance and durability.

Innovators of differentiated products in the downstream space will seek to protect and monetise their innovation. They will also need to ensure that they have freedom to operate for all the products in their extensive product portfolios.

2.1 How should I protect products resulting from collaborative development?

Many differentiated products will have resulted from collaborative efforts and may have resulted from open innovation. These types of innovation can result in the rapid development of technically superior products but can present challenges when seeking to protect the resulting innovation.

Ownership of IP typically flows from inventorship. Article 60(1) of the European Patent Convention states that the right to a European patent shall belong to the inventor or his successor in title. The US patent statute[16] states that a person to whom the inventor has assigned or is under an obligation to assign the invention may make an application for patent. If inventors are employed, the rights in the invention typically pass to the employer, either by law or by virtue of an employment agreement. In a scenario where there are multiple inventors employed by different organisations, then the typical legal outcome, in the absence of any agreement to the contrary, is for any arising IP to be co-owned by the different organisations.

Co-ownership of IP such as patents is legally complicated and, in almost all cases, it is preferable to avoid co-ownership. One problem with co-ownership is that the legal rights of co-owners are different in different jurisdictions, and it can be easy for co-owners to assume that the rights that they have in one jurisdiction are also available in another jurisdiction. For example, co-owners in the US can license a patent independently from the other co-owners, whereas in many other jurisdictions such as the UK, consent is required from all co-owners before a licence can be granted. Another issue with co-ownership is that you may not be able to enforce the patent rights without the cooperation of all the co-owners. In the US, all co-owners must join in enforcement actions.

The parties developing differentiated products in the downstream space are generally sophisticated in their approach and will seek to clarify the rights and obligations of all parties at the outset of any collaboration. Such an agreement will address the ownership of any IP (including know-how and inventions) that results from the collaboration and will address the rights that the different parties have to use background IP and arising IP. This avoids the default co-ownership position and ensures that the agreed ownership and use rights reflect the commercial objectives of the different parties. It is common to specify different rights and obligations in different fields of use. For example, in a collaborative development for a new fuel additive an additive manufacturer might acquire rights to make and sell the additive, an oil major might acquire rights to use the additive and to sell fuels incorporating the additive, and a university might acquire rights to use the additive in research and to publish results based on such research. Or, in a collaborative development for a new lubricant, a first company might acquire rights to use the additive and sell lubricants for marine applications and a second company might acquire rights to use the additive and sell lubricants for industrial applications.

2.2 How do I protect innovative products resulting from open innovation?

In this section, we use a case study to illustrate the challenges of developing an IP strategy to support product development carried out using an open innovation model. The case study shows that it is possible to adopt an open innovation approach whilst protecting the innovation resulting from that approach.

Case study: Lubricants IP strategy development

Yann Cramer currently holds executive and non-executive roles at innovative start-up enterprises. He lectures at the Ecole Supérieure des Sciences Economiques et Commerciales (ESSEC) and Paris I Panthéon-Sorbonne University on entrepreneurship, intrapreneurship and innovation management. He was formerly the head of Shell's Lubricant Discovery Hub. We asked Yann to give his thoughts on formulating an IP strategy when conducting research and development via an open innovation strategy.

Why did the Lubricants Discovery Hub adopt an open innovation strategy?

We were seeking diversity and speed. A large organisation such as Shell has many technical experts, but it can be difficult to mobilise such experts at short notice. Open innovation provides immediate access to experts from a diverse range of disciplines with a diverse range of thought processes. Once a challenge has been adequately framed, this can accelerate innovation, particularly at the initial ideas-generation stage. Such acceleration is highly valuable in the race to get to market.

What were the priorities of your IP strategy?

The primary objective was to preserve freedom to operate. We wanted to avoid a situation where a product is ready to launch, but competitor patents prevent you from launching; often when the competitor does not even have a product on the market.

We viewed patents as strategic tools, not as trophies in the cupboard. New developments were reported quickly and we used a decision tree to assess whether or not we needed to file a patent application, make a (non-patent) public disclosure or maintain the information as a trade secret. The decision-making criteria included the strategic fit of the technology, the size of market opportunity and our ability to provide data to support a patent filing. People often expect that the trade secret option should be the default, but keeping a secret from being divulged is much harder than people imagine. In fact, making public disclosures – in order to preserve freedom to operate – has to be the default option. Also, when we did decide to seek a patent application, we didn't focus on producing 'gold-plated' patent applications; we simply ensured that we could properly define the invention and that there was a prospect of producing supporting data during the priority year.

We always considered that speed beats secrecy. Being the first to market is often a more effective barrier to market entry for competitors than patents. Patent protection can slow down competitors but they usually have options for designing around the patents. It is like a game of Mario Kart – you can throw a lot of banana skins (patents) to slow down your competitors, but ultimately you need to be in front to win the race.

How did you address the IP challenges of the open innovation model?
Many R&D organisations are reluctant to engage with open innovation, and IP issues are cited as a reason not to use an open innovation approach. However, we made sure that the 'rules of the game' were clear to all contributors right from the start. It was important to choose the right partners and have clarity from the beginning on the ownership of IP and the procedures for protecting that IP. Many partners are not interested in ownership of IP; that is not their priority. It was easy and quick to negotiate suitable agreements with such partners.

Co-development – where you don't stop at idea generation, but co-develop a new product all the way to market – is more complicated than open innovation. With co-development, you need to consider how the proprietary results are going to be treated. However, it is still possible to reach a mutually beneficial agreement, particularly when the parties have a sophisticated understanding of IP and are clear on their commercial objectives.[17]

2.3 What are the IP challenges when considering freedom to operate for a large portfolio of differentiated products?

The purpose of any freedom to operate assessment is to ensure that there are no third-party IP rights that will limit your operations in your chosen markets. With a single product or process, this can be a difficult exercise; you might have to consider the scope and validity of multiple third-party patent rights across multiple territories. With a large portfolio of differentiated products, this assessment can become considerably more difficult as you consider multiple formulations and even greater numbers of potentially relevant patents across multiple territories.

Freedom to operate is primarily about managing risk, and when assessing your portfolio of products, you can take a risk-based approach. The risk of being sued for patent infringement will be lower if a product has already been on the market for a long time, or if it was described in a publicly available document many years ago. The risk of patent infringement will be higher if the product has been recently launched (or is about to be launched) and contains components that you know to be highly innovative. You should also consider: (1) the nature of your competitors; (2) the territories in which you are operating; and (3) the similarity of your products to competitor products. If you are launching a product similar to that of a litigious competitor in a country where patent litigation is common, you will need to carry out a detailed and rigorous freedom to operate assessment. You may be able to take a different approach if you a launching a product that is dissimilar to competitor products

"A fundamentally important feature of any freedom to operate assessment is to obtain detailed and accurate descriptions of the products and the processes for making those products."

in a country where cooperative settlements are more common than litigation.

A fundamentally important feature of any freedom to operate assessment is to obtain detailed and accurate descriptions of the products and the processes for making those products. A single change in a product formulation (eg, substitution of one component for a similar component or a slight increase in the amount of one component) or in a process scheme (eg, switching the type of catalyst that is used or omitting a purification step) can completely change the outcome of the assessment. It is important to explain this significance to those providing the product and process descriptions and to ensure that any changes are reported in a timely manner.

One particular challenge with downstream products is that they may contain proprietary additives, supplied by a third party. You may not be able to carry out a meaningful freedom to operate assessment if you do not have information on the chemical nature of the additives. There are a number of ways of solving this issue. Your additive supplier may be willing to divulge the details of the additive to a legal practitioner under conditions of confidentiality for the sole purpose of carrying out the freedom to operate assessment. Alternatively, your additive supplier may be willing to provide an indemnity in relation to patent infringement for formulations containing the additive. With this solution, you will need to ensure that the value of the indemnity is appropriate considering the potential liability for patent infringement.

If your freedom to operate assessment uncovers third-party patent rights that appear potentially relevant to your products, you will need to consider how to address this. If the scope of the patent is of concern, but there are reasons for challenging the validity of the patent, then you may wish to launch a legal challenge to the validity of the patent. Legal challenges are available in national courts but there are also post-grant review procedures at many patent offices. In Europe, it is possible to file an opposition against the grant of a patent in a nine-month period after the grant of a European patent. In the US, it is possible to launch proceedings before the Patent Trial and Appeal Board (PTAB) either as a post-grant review (within nine months of grant) or as an *inter partes* review (after nine months of grant). If the validity of the patent seems robust, then you can consider approaching the patent owner for a licence or can consider possibilities for designing around the scope of the claims.

3. Conclusion

Downstream innovation continues to provide improved processes and products, offering better performance, efficiency and

"Downstream innovation continues to provide improved processes and products, offering better performance, efficiency and sustainability."

sustainability. A carefully considered IP strategy is a critical tool for ensuring that you can exploit and monetise your innovative technology.

Notes

1 Article 28 1(b) of the Agreement on Trade-Related Aspects of Intellectual Property Rights (as amended by the 2005 Protocol), www.wto.org/english/docs_e/legal_e/trips_e.htm#fntext-7.
2 *Nalco Co v Chem-Mod LLC*, 883 F.3d 1337 (Fed. Cir. 2018), https://caselaw.findlaw.com/us-federal-circuit/1890589.html.
3 *Ibid.*
4 *Ibid.*
5 *Travel Sentry Inc v Tropp*, 877 F.3d 1370 (Fed. Cir. 2017), https://caselaw.findlaw.com/us-federal-circuit/1883409.html.
6 *Ibid.*
7 *Ibid.*
8 *Ibid.*
9 *Ibid.*
10 *Pioneer Electronics Capital Inc v Warner Music Manufacturing GmbH* [1995] RPC 487.
11 *Medimmune Ltd v Novartis Pharmaceuticals UK Ltd* [2011] EWHC 1669 (Pat).
12 35 USC 271(g).
13 *Syngenta Crop Protection LLC v Willowood LLC*, 944 F.3d 1344 (Fed. Cir. 2019), https://cafc.uscourts.gov/sites/default/files/opinions-orders/18-1614.Opinion.12-18-2019.pdf.
14 *Ibid.*
15 *Ibid.*
16 35 USC 118.
17 Thank you to Yann Cramer for his time and for sharing his expertise on the subject of open innovation and IP strategy in a downstream business.

"Environmental, social and governance issues are now very high on the corporate agenda. There is growing pressure from investors and the broader stakeholders of the traditional energy majors – and even from the courts in some countries – to set earlier and more ambitious lowered emissions targets."

III. Renewables: solar – spotlight on BNRG

Eoin Langford
BNRG Renewables Ltd
Jon Moorhouse
Keystone Law

1. Introduction

Environmental, social and governance issues are now very high on the corporate agenda. There is growing pressure from investors and the broader stakeholders of the traditional energy majors – and even from the courts in some countries[1] – to set earlier and more ambitious lowered emissions targets.

Renewable energy sources constitute an increasingly significant part of the energy mix. Intellectual property (IP) plays a key role in enabling renewables companies to protect their investments, maximise business returns and differentiate themselves to win and preserve business opportunities in a fiercely competitive market.

Nowhere more so than in solar, where photovoltaic cell and other component costs continue to fall and margins are extremely tight. A 2020 World Intellectual Property Organization (WIPO) study[2] found that over half of renewables-related patent applications were in relation to solar: twice as many as the next largest renewables area, wind.

In this chapter, we will focus on solar energy, looking at the different elements of the supply chain project life cycle, and showcasing BNRG Renewables Ltd (BNRG) – a solar energy company that is going from strength-to-strength – to illustrate the role IP plays.

Alongside patents, many renewables companies will use – and carefully protect – trade secrets and confidential information concerning various aspects of the relevant hardware and how they manufacture and deploy it. This could be: (1) confidential design documents; (2) the results of data interpretation and analysis; or (3) the algorithms and software developed to interpret and analyse data.

2. Hardware

2.1 The technology

Interview with Andre Lopes (BNRG Engineer), Hugo Diepman BNRG Engineer) and Richard Jackson (BNRG Asset Manager)

Q: Can you briefly explain the technology underpinning solar energy generation?
The Sun is constantly emitting energy in the form of sunlight which we call irradiance. This irradiance reaches the solar panels and is converted into direct current (DC) by the solar cells. This electrical energy is combined and is sent to an inverter. The inverter converts the direct current into alternating current (AC). From there, the AC goes to a transformer and on to the utility grid for use.

Q: What components/hardware are involved?
Solar panels are, of course, central to a solar facility. The panels are held in place using steel racking. Inverters are key also. Transformers are used to match the inverter voltage with the grid's required output. Breakers and switchgear are also used to provide electrical protection systems for both personnel and the equipment.

Q: What role, if any, does software play?
Software has several applications in solar generation, for example, it is used to:

- Identify how many panels can be installed on the site.
- Determine how steep, and in which direction, the slopes are.
- Determine how much energy the project is expected to generate.
- Monitor real-time and historic power-generation data. For site performance and status reports, we use a SCADA (supervisory control and data acquisition) software. This software is important, as it allows asset managers to collect key data and allows the operation and maintenance contractors to remotely monitor the system without the need for a physical presence on site. Software can vary depending on the portfolio.

"Alongside patents, many renewables companies will use – and carefully protect – trade secrets and confidential information concerning various aspects of the relevant hardware and how they manufacture and deploy it."

Q: Do you ever use sensors (eg, with real-time data feeds) for predictive maintenance?
Yes, we do use real-time sensor data to provide maintenance predictions. Currently, it's fairly minor stuff, such as sensors to identify when panels need to be cleaned in the future, plus inverter or transformer cooling issues. However, this is increased where we analyse current trends against previous historical data to evaluate if a system will require additional maintenance prior to its planned schedule and to identify potential failures for the future.

Q: What innovations/improvements have you seen recently or do you foresee?
Module manufacturers are constantly innovating in order to achieve higher efficiencies. Solar panel efficiency refers to how much light energy a solar panel converts into electricity. Two innovations on the horizon are heterojunction modules and N-type modules.

The current trend in utility-scale solar generation is to go bigger. Panel manufacturers are trying to get higher and higher watt (W) classes. Sites that we built in 2018/2019 used 315W to 325W panels, sites that we are constructing today are using 400W to 450W panels and, today, there are panels on the market which are 600W and higher. Current modules use a cell technology called

P-Type Mono PERC. This technology is reaching the limit of its theoretical efficiency. So, in order to achieve higher powers, the modules are actually getting physically bigger. The modules we used on our sites built in 2018/2019 were about 2 metres long, whereas the 600W modules are about 2.4 metres long. Due to the P-Type Mono PERC cells reaching their theoretical efficiency limit, manufacturers are looking to other cell technologies as mentioned above. The ones that seem to be next up are TOPCon and HJT. Slightly further out are technologies utilising Perovskite, Tandem and Hybrids.

The capacity of inverters is also increasing. Where we were previously seeing string inverters of 125kW (kilowatts), we are now seeing 250kW to 350kW string inverters. We have heard whispers of a 1MW (megawatt) string inverter. It will be interesting to see where manufacturers start drawing the line between string inverters and central inverters. Central inverters are increasing in size as well. We have just built sites (2021) using 2.5MW central inverters. Recently when designing a site using the same inverter, we were told by the manufacturer they were no longer offering technical support for it. Currently, on the market we are seeing central inverters from 3.1MW to 7.2MW.

Racking has to just keep up with the size of modules. Also, what we're starting to see here is that as less 'good' land is available, the supporting structure has to start dealing with poorer quality land.

Improvements in storage (batteries etc) and linking solar facilities with green hydrogen is probably the next big shift as more and more solar comes onto the grid.

As grids, globally, become decentralised and non-synchronous we see a greater emphasis on renewable generation systems providing the necessary grid stability associated with the current trend. As a result, solar sites will be required to provide more reactive power and frequency response solutions which can be achieved by utilising more advanced inverters and storage systems.

Q: Do you ever encounter patent or trade secret issues from your suppliers, partners or competitors?

Different aspects of the technology, such as racking systems, are certainly patented.[3] However, we buy our hardware from suppliers and do not usually encounter any patent issues.

In relation to trade secrets and confidential information, we will always be careful not to share our workflows, algorithms or software with competitors as this can help distinguish us from other solar companies when bidding for new projects.

Figure 1. Cross section of panel on a mount/link to inverter (1)

Source: © 2021 BNRG Renewables Ltd

Figure 2. Cross section of panel on a mount/link to inverter (2)

Source: © 2021 BNRG Renewables Ltd

2.2 Manufacture

Manufacturers are often located in territories where there are lower cost bases and many solar companies in Europe or North America may import the hardware they need.

The manufacturers may well have IP rights relating to the different components they make, for example, in the inverters, racking or modules: these rights could be in relation to particular products or to the processes used to manufacture the products.[4]

The fundamental technology may not be new, but there are continual improvements, bringing improved performance, cost-efficiency and so on.

In addition, companies in this part of the supply chain will most likely have substantial know-how and trade secrets relating to optimal, cost-efficient, reliable and safe manufacturing techniques and processes.

2.3 Procurement

Like many solar companies, BNRG does not manufacture hardware but has procurement contracts with relevant manufacturers or suppliers.

Interview with Eoin Langford (BNRG Head of Legal) and Leonardo Azevedo (BNRG Head of Procurement)

Q: To what extent do you need to expressly deal with IP licensing when buying in the kit you need?
This is not a concern at this time. It is standard for solar equipment supply agreements to contain licences to import, install and use etc the equipment. However, should we decide to self-perform the operation and maintenance activities at our solar facilities, we may need to acquire software licensing rights for plant monitoring software.

Q: Do you perceive BNRG has significant exposure to potential claims of IP infringement from third parties (eg, other manufacturers)?
Not at this time. These kinds of claims are rare in the marketplace. The applicable technologies are well-established. That said, there is also much innovation in the marketplace – such as developing bifacial modules and higher watt classes. However, there does not appear to be a litigious culture amongst manufacturers in the sector.

Q: How do you address this (eg, indemnities and warranties claims)?
We aim to put in place IP infringement indemnities in supplier and EPC (engineering, procurement and construction) agreements. The effect of these indemnities is that, in case a supplier or contractor is acting in breach of a third party's IP rights or causing BNRG to act in breach of such rights, we are not at risk of being sued.

Q: Do you deal with software separately?
Yes.

Q: Would this typically be proprietary to the manufacturers (eg, firmware) or are there specialist solar software companies?
This would most typically be proprietary to manufacturers and would be procured through the EPC contractor. Where the EPC contractor's licensing agreements expire, BNRG then procures the software. However, this is not always done as projects can be, and have been, sold prior to the expiry of the licensing arrangements between the EPC contractor and software company.

Q: To what extent is any relevant software simply open source?
We don't foresee any piece of software we may need in the future for plant monitoring being open source.

3. Project development and asset management

BNRG then has in-house know-how in market selection, site selection and design optimisation to leverage in order to differentiate BNRG from the competition.

3.1 Site selection and design optimisation

There is significant know-how and experience in how to assess markets (eg, available grid capacity, demand for solar, supply of competing (perhaps traditional hydrocarbon) energy sources, political and regulatory transparency and stability, capacity of current distribution network, local environmental and geographical challenges and so on) and how to balance and mitigate risks across different territories.

Figure 3. Completed solar facility

Source: © 2021 BNRG Renewables Ltd

Interview with Andre Lopes (BNRG Engineer) and Hugo Diepman (BNRG Engineer)

Q: What are the key considerations when designing an array for a new project?
There are several factors which influence BNRG's site selection process.

We need to check if the site is flat enough to accommodate the racking for the solar panels and if the site is clear of major obstructions.

Proximity to the utility grid is very important from engineering, commercial and legal standpoints. Relatedly, an important factor is whether the grid has available capacity to accommodate the project without major upgrades. Whether the site is big enough according to the grid voltage nearby and the amount of energy which the site is expected to generate are also considered.

Environmental and planning issues also figure in site selection. For example, if there are wetlands on site these pose development challenges.

Q: How would you say your approach differentiates BNRG from competitors?
In BNRG, we have the expertise to assess sites against all of the above factors in a preliminary manner in-house. This allows us to check those items early in the development process at a low cost and to proceed only with projects that have good potential for successful development.

Q: Do you ever seek patent protection for any of your ideas?
Not at the moment. We would keep our know-how confidential to the company and ensure this is not shared with competitors.

Q: 'Crystal balling' – do you ever use patent searching and analysis as a tool to understand future developments?
We don't do this. Such technology would be too far in the future for our processes. We tend to look two to three years ahead when assessing future possibilities.

Q: Would you say BNRG is a first or early adopter of technologies, or do you prefer to wait until proven?
We are an early adopter of technologies. Although we adopt technology early, we always conduct due diligence on our side, in conjunction with the manufacturers, to allow us to get comfortable with the product.

We are also a pioneer in solar markets. For example, BNRG is currently constructing some of the first-ever solar facilities in the Republic of Ireland. Thus, we are comfortable not only in adopting new tech, but also in applying existing tech to novel market and geographical conditions.

3.2 EPC and partnering

Solar companies will often collaborate with partners: perhaps for site selection and/or design optimisation, and then engaging EPC contractors for project development.

Interview with Eoin Langford (BNRG Head of Legal)

Q: How is in-house know-how protected when engaging EPC contractors?

Contractual protection. We will ensure we have in place appropriate confidentiality clauses to prevent the contractors from sharing our designs and know-how with our competitors, requiring them to only use the information on the project for us, and requiring them to delete all records of the relevant confidential information at the end of the project.

Q: To what extent do you share critical modelling techniques, know-how or other key aspects underlying BNRG's business model? (eg, restricted personnel only, most confidential, encryption or access on site only)

We actually share most if not all our modelling techniques in terms of energy modelling since we want the EPC contractor and investors to see the project as well as we see it, and this is where the confidentiality and restricted use provisions in our EPC agreements play an essential role, ensuring they can only use these techniques on the relevant projects for BNRG.

Q: Do you ever consider the risk of contamination of BNRG's know-how with information received on a confidential basis from contractors? (This would be where such information received gets mixed up with your own information and you have to keep the whole lot secret to avoid being in breach of BNRG's confidentiality obligations, which may impact on your ability to exploit/publish/patent any of your own inventions or ideas.)

This has not come up as an issue in practice as yet, but we are investigating ways to protect any IP that we create in collaboration with our development partners, for example, bespoke project management systems.

Q: Do you license your own IP or sub-license (eg, hardware/ software IP) to contractors or license in from contractors?
No, except in so far as we share confidential information with them on a restricted use basis, where they can only use our information for the purposes of carrying out the project for us.

4. Reputation and brand management
As for any industry, protection and exploitation of the business brand can foster generate greater customer awareness and loyalty.

Interview with David Maguire (BNRG Founder and Director) and Richard Jackson (BNRG Asset Manager)

Q: How important is your brand and reputation to your company's success?
BNRG's reputation as the only full life cycle solar firm that provides knowledge, trust and flexibility for its partners is of great value to our business. Deep partnerships and real relationships have always formed the basis of our business model and they continue to inform our operations internationally. With a global mindset and local approach, BNRG brings trust, expertise and a personal touch to all our dealings, ensuring the highest standards in green energy can work, and can be affordable, wherever we operate. In an expanding global market, which values dependability, ethics and a personal relationship, these aspects of our business help to set us apart.

Our logo, as the 'face' of our business, is also important to our success. It's what people instantly recognise. Our branding creates trust, builds financial value to our business and inspires our employees.

Q: What actions do you undertake to develop, preserve and enhance your reputation?
We have registered our name and logo as trademarks in Ireland – our core territory – in order to protect our brand, and will consider registering in other territories as well, going forward.

Our interactions with the communities in which we develop solar farms are crucial for maintaining and strengthening our reputation. We are keen to ensure that all stakeholders have positive experiences with BNRG Ltd which they can share with others. For example, in Ireland, we aim to hold town hall-style meetings before making our planning application submissions. During the last year, this was not possible due to COVID-19. Instead, we sent out leaflets to local residents where we were progressing a planning application. We also publish a statement in the local newspaper whenever an application is being submitted.

BNRG's involvement with the Irish Solar Energy Association (ISEA) also protects our reputation. The ISEA is a non-profit solar trade organisation which was founded in 2013. BNRG was a founding member and we have been actively involved ever since. BNRG staff are involved in running the organisation, they participate in panel discussions and they contribute to policy formation and advocacy. The ISEA was founded in order to advance a policy and regulatory landscape promoting solar power as a leading renewable energy technology that will decarbonise Ireland's electricity system and contribute to a strong and sustainable economy. The ISEA works closely with government departments and other significant state agencies to advance the solar agenda on behalf of its members. As members of Solar Power Europe, the ISEA drives the Irish solar agenda at the highest levels in Brussels, from the European Commission to the various Directorates General. An important example of the ISEA's activities is the grid working group which aims to develop and advance policy in relation to solar electricity and the national grid.

Reputation management is not the primary reason for BNRG's involvement with the ISEA; we are involved to support the development of solar photoelectric facilities in Ireland. Our involvement does nonetheless strengthen our reputation. It improves the visibility of our brand, allows us to stand out as an industry leader and enables us to strengthen our relationships with industry colleagues.

Q: Have you ever had any issues of people seeking to pass themselves off as BNRG, using your trademark or doing anything that impacts on your brand?
No, thankfully.

Notes

1 https://uitspraken.rechtspraak.nl/inziendocument?id=ECLI:NL:RBDHA:2021:5339: The Hague District Court order on Royal Dutch Shell (RDS) in May 2021 to reduce group CO2 emissions by 45% in 2030, compared to 2019 levels.
2 James Nurton (WIPO), "Patenting Trends in Renewable Energy" (March 2020), www.wipo.int/wipo_magazine/en/2020/01/article_0008.html.
3 See, eg, European Patent Office (EPO), "US9328942 (B1) – Solar Panel Racking System", https://worldwide.espacenet.com/publicationDetails/biblio?FT=D&date=20160503&DB=&locale=en_EP&CC=US&NR=9328942B1&KC=B1&ND=4.
4 See, eg, US8542512B2: improved techniques for manufacturing power conditioning units (inverters) for use with photovoltaic (PV) modules, and inverters manufactured using these techniques, https://patents.google.com/patent/US8542512B2/en?oq=US8542512B2.

"The energy industry, like many others, is undergoing the monumental change of digitalising existing processes and incorporating artificial intelligence (AI) into all aspects of the industry. This transition comes at a critical time."

IV. Digitalisation

Charles T Collins-Chase
Kathryn R Judson
Paul Townsend
Finnegan LLP

1. Digitalisation and artificial intelligence are rapidly changing the energy industry

The energy industry, like many others, is undergoing the monumental change of digitalising existing processes and incorporating artificial intelligence (AI) into all aspects of the industry. This transition comes at a critical time. World energy consumption increased by over 28,000 TWh (roughly 21%) from 2009 to 2019.[1] The increase was even larger in the renewable energy sector, which saw nearly a 71% increase over that same period.[2] This growth, coupled with increased regulation and consumer demand for products that are shifting energy consumption (eg, electric vehicles (EVs)), underscore the importance of digitalisation and AI to help the industry adapt and prosper.[3]

Digital technologies are not new to the energy industry. Grid management was digitalised long ago, and oil and gas companies have used digital model exploration technologies for decades.[4] The pace of innovation in AI and digitalisation has increased, however, and recent advances have provided tremendous benefits to the industry in terms of efficiency and safety. For example, ExxonMobil worked with the Massachusetts Institute of Technology (MIT) to create self-learning, submersible robots for safe and efficient offshore drilling and production operations.[5] Shell uses AI to help guide drills as they move through the subsurface by applying algorithms derived from historical drilling data and simulated exploration, including subsurface data from seismic surveys and mechanical information from the drill bit.[6] Shell also relies on AI to improve safety for some dangerous tasks, such as using an automated pipe handler on Shell's 120,000-ton Olympus platform to avoid human workers handling 300-pound sections of drill pipe.[7]

These advances are also helping shape other parts of the energy sector outside of exploration and production. General Electric (GE), for example, is building a machine learning framework – called Pro-ML-IDeAS – that uses an AI-driven invertible neural network to generate engineering designs for aerodynamic systems, enabling more optimised designs for industrial gas turbine aerodynamic components.[8] Xcel Energy is using eSmart Systems' AI-based analytics to enhance aerial inspection of Xcel's transmission grid using unmanned drones, reducing operation costs, decreasing failure rates and extending asset life.[9] IBM developed a solar forecasting program for the US Department of Energy's SunShot Initiative[10] by combining self-learning weather models, data sets of historical weather data, real-time measurement from local weather stations, sensor networks and cloud information from satellite imaging and sky cameras.[11] IBM's programme resulted in a 30% improvement in the accuracy of the solar forecasting.[12]

These examples only scratch the surface of the possibilities for the energy industry. AI and digital technologies can also be used to predict demand spikes and capacity levels, remotely monitor existing oil rigs, create predictive models to assess potential impacts of new developments and analyse geophysical data to find new exploration opportunities. Further, these technologies can also enable autonomous and self-learning systems that make better safety decisions and protect workers.

These advances in digitalisation and AI are expected to provide enormous financial benefits. The World Economic Forum estimates that digitalisation can unlock around US$1.6 trillion in value for oil and gas companies.[13] Industry analysts at McKinsey believe that digital technologies can reduce capital expenditures by up to 20%, as well as cut upstream operating costs by 3% to 5% and downstream operating costs by half as much.[14] The International Energy Agency states that digitalisation could decrease production costs for oil and gas companies by between 10% to 20%.[15] For power generation, digitalisation could save up to US$80 billion per year globally.[16] Smart demand response could save approximately US$270 billion in new electricity infrastructure by providing up to 185 GW of system flexibility.[17] It does not stop there. By using digitalisation to help integrate variable renewables into energy grids by using weather

"The fourth industrial revolution is underway, and the energy industry is taking full advantage of it. As with any monumental industrial shift, innovation is leading the way."

forecasting, the EU alone could reduce curtailment of solar and wind power (ie, reducing output below what the resource could have produced) from 7% to 1.6% in 2040, which would avoid up to 30 million tons of CO_2 emissions.[18] And the list goes on.

The fourth industrial revolution is underway, and the energy industry is taking full advantage of it. As with any monumental industrial shift, innovation is leading the way. So, what intellectual property (IP) challenges do innovators of digital and AI energy technologies face?

2. Potential intellectual property issues facing AI and digital innovations

2.1 Patent eligibility

Innovators of digital and AI energy technologies face many technical IP challenges, and patent eligibility of digital inventions has created one of the biggest obstacles. In the US, digital innovations are frequently struck down under 35 USC §101, a provision of the patent law that has been used to bar certain categories of inventions from receiving patent protection. In theory, the plain text of the statute broadly permits patents on "any new and useful process, machine, manufacture, or composition of matter". Despite this broad definition, however, the US Supreme Court has recognised several judicial exceptions under the statute, which bar claims directed to abstract ideas, laws of nature or natural phenomenon. Under the Supreme Court's two-part test from *Alice Corp Pty Ltd v CLS Bank International*,[19] a claim is ineligible under §101 where (1) it is "directed to" a law of nature, natural phenomenon or abstract idea and (2) the claim elements, considered "both individually and 'as an ordered combination'", are insufficient to "'transform the nature of the claim' into a patent-eligible application".

Since the US Supreme Court's 2014 ruling in *Alice*, §101 has been used to invalidate numerous patents on digital technology and artificial intelligence as directed to no more than an abstract idea. Even patent claims that involve tangible, physical elements sometimes face the same fate. In *Electric Power Group LLC v Alstom SA*,[20] for example, the US Court of Appeals for the Federal Circuit upheld a district court decision invalidating claims directed to automatically analysing events in real time on an interconnected power grid to generate a composite indicator of grid reliability.

In Europe, inventions in all fields of technology are patentable provided they are new, involve an inventive step and are industrially applicable, as defined by Article 52(1) of the European Patent Convention.

"Different national patent offices have reached different conclusions about whether an AI system can be an inventor."

European case law further explains that an invention must have technical character and provide a technical effect. Article 52(2) defines excluded matter such as mathematical models, computer programs, scientific discoveries, business methods and the like. Article 52(3) states that the exclusion only applies to the extent that the patent or application relates to such subject matter or activities "as such". In practice, the exclusion can be overcome if an invention provides a technical effect (ie, a technical solution to a technical problem). According to Section G-II-3.3.1 of the European Patent Office (EPO) Guidelines for Examination, AI is treated as a mathematical model or computer-implemented invention. So, for AI to be patentable, it must provide some type of technical effect.

2.2 Patent inventorship

Digital and AI technologies face other patent law issues as well, including who should be considered the inventor of innovations developed wholly or partly by AI systems. Different national patent offices have reached different conclusions about whether an AI system can be an inventor. In the US, the United States Patent and Trademark Office (USPTO) resolved this issue, in part, in an April 2020 decision, concluding that only a natural person (and not an AI system) can be the inventor of a patent.[21] The case involved two patent applications that listed as the sole inventor an AI system called DABUS (Device for the Autonomous Bootstrapping of Unified Sentience). The DABUS machine allegedly invented the subject matter of the two applications without human input or intervention. The USPTO rejected the applications for failure to properly identify an inventor, reasoning that the Patent Act repeatedly refers to an "inventor" as a natural person and citing Federal Circuit case law rejecting the premise that corporations or states could be inventors.[22] Similar applications had also been filed in the UK Intellectual Property Office (UKIPO) and the EPO, which both rejected the applications because they failed to name a human as an inventor.[23, 24] Notably, however, both the UKIPO and the EPO seem to have accepted, without substantive analysis, that DABUS had created the inventions.[25] But recently, the South African Patent Office granted a similar patent conceived by the same DABUS system, showing that different countries will respond to AI-based inventions differently.[26]

In October 2020, the USPTO issued a 56-page report titled "Public Views on Artificial Intelligence and Intellectual Property Policy", which provided a more detailed look into the public's view on AI in IP.[27] One of the general themes was that artificial general intelligence (AGI) – intelligence on the same level as that possessed by humans – "had not yet arrived" and, therefore, that "AI could neither invent nor author without human intervention".[28] Although the report viewed current AI systems as not being eligible as inventors, it left open the possibility of AGI being eligible as an inventor.

For now, it appears that only human beings will be granted patents. But questions for AI-generated innovations remain. In cases where an AI system truly generates a portion of an invention autonomously, for example, could the patents be subject to an inventorship challenge alleging that the named human inventor(s) did not truly conceive the full scope of the claimed invention? If an AI system autonomously creates a part of an invention, will that invention be subject to an obviousness/inventive step challenge on the grounds that the AI system's work was routine optimisation? Because many questions have not yet been answered, companies must exercise caution by looking for human inventors for AI-assisted innovations, drafting patent claims strategically to focus on human-invented subject matter, and including inventive elements that are not simply optimisation of known parameters.

Patent offices around the world have recognised the need for specific AI policies. South Korea's Intellectual Property Office (KIPO), for example, met with the USPTO to discuss "developing new collaborative efforts amid [the ongoing] accelerated digital transformation trend".[29] The China National Intellectual Property Administration (CNIPA) revised its patent examination guidelines in November 2020 to address issues with AI-related inventions.[30] The Japanese Patent Office (JPO) also released a report on trends in AI-related patenting, demonstrating a significant increase in AI-based patents over the past five years.[31]

The efforts by national patent offices to adapt policies to handle AI and digital innovations could not come at a better time. According to the World Intellectual Property Organization (WIPO), of the nearly 340,000 patent applications on AI technologies that have been filed since 1960, over half have been filed since 2013.[32] The pace of AI-based patent filings is growing particularly fast in certain sub-areas. Machine learning, the dominant technique disclosed in AI patents, saw average annual growth in patent filings of 28% from 2013 to 2016.[33] Within machine learning, neural network filings increased by an average of 46% over the same period, while deep learning saw an enormous average annual growth in patent filings of 175%.[34] Filings for robotics and control methods saw a 55% average annual growth.[35] One thing is clear: patenting rates for AI-based inventions are growing far faster than for other technologies.

2.3 Trade secret protection

Patents are not the only way to protect digital and AI-related innovations in the energy industry. Trade secrets are valuable and sometimes a more suitable form of protection. In general, confidential information that gives your company a competitive advantage may qualify as a trade secret, as long as it is not generally known or readily ascertainable by proper means, and provided that you use reasonable measures to maintain its secrecy. Trade secrets, therefore, are an important complement to patents and should be part of a comprehensive IP strategy for protecting digital- and AI-based innovations.

Trade secret law can provide significant protection even where a patent may be difficult or impossible to obtain, such as for inventions that are likely to face a patent-eligibility challenge. The passage of the Defend Trade Secrets Act (DTSA) in the US in 2016 has made trade secret protection even more appealing. The DTSA sets out statutory requirements for trade secret protection and provides trade secret owners with a federal cause of action for trade secret misappropriation, which was previously subject to state-by-state variations in trade secret law.[36]

Whereas a patent provides protection for a limited period, trade secrets can last as long as the information remains secret and the owner uses reasonable measures to maintain secrecy. Thus, trade secrets can potentially provide long-lasting protection for AI innovations and other digital technologies when publicly disclosing the information in a patent would diminish its value. Trade secrets

"Patents are not the only way to protect digital and AI-related innovations in the energy industry. Trade secrets are valuable and sometimes a more suitable form of protection."

also avoid the potentially years-long prosecution that is often necessary to obtain a patent. Instead, trade secrets provide protection immediately without the need for public disclosure or costly patent prosecution fees.

Trade secret protection does have potential drawbacks, however. Most notably, trade secret owners may be left with no recourse if another party obtains the trade secret through legitimate means, such as reverse engineering, independent invention or accidental disclosure by the owner. Indeed, companies sometimes face a situation where technology maintained as a trade secret is independently developed and patented by a competitor, creating a freedom to operate risk. Moreover, a trade secret, unlike a patent, does not give its owner an exclusive monopoly over the subject matter of the trade secret – the secret is only protected against misappropriation. Companies often encounter difficulties both in properly maintaining the required secrecy and in proving misappropriation. These difficulties may arise from: (1) the volume of proprietary information that a typical energy company possesses; (2) the mobility of the workforce; (3) the growing importance of energy industry collaborations (eg, joint ventures) in which companies share information with potential competitors; and (4) omissions in confidentiality agreements governing trade secrets.

3. Patents: common issues and strategies

3.1 Strategies for overcoming patent-eligibility challenges

As discussed at section 2.1, the US Supreme Court's decision in *Alice* holds that an invention directed to an abstract idea can only be patent eligible if it supplies an "inventive concept" sufficient to transform the claim into something "significantly more" than any underlying abstract idea.[37] Implementing an invention on a general-purpose computer is insufficient to transform an abstract idea into a patent-eligible invention.[38]

The US Supreme Court's guidance has ultimately led to confusion, including in the energy industry, regarding what it means for an invention to be "directed to" an abstract idea and what sort of "inventive concept" is sufficient to transform an underlying abstract idea into a patent-eligible application of that idea. The energy industry traditionally faced fewer patent-eligibility challenges than other industries because innovations largely were tied to physical objects or processes. In recent years, however, the increasing pace of digital and AI innovation in the energy industry has led to more patent-eligibility challenges. Luckily, earlier cases in the industry provide some guidance about drafting claims to withstand such a challenge.

In *Electric Power Group v Alstom*, the Federal Circuit found that the

"Implementing an invention on a general-purpose computer is insufficient to transform an abstract idea into a patent-eligible invention."

claims at issue, directed to systems and methods for monitoring the performance of an electric power grid in real time, failed to describe more than collecting data from multiple sources, analysing the data and displaying the results.[39] The court thus held that the claims were "directed to" an abstract idea under *Alice* step one, reasoning that the collection, analysis and display of information was squarely in "a familiar class of claims 'directed to' a patent ineligible concept".[40] The Federal Circuit further explained that, although the claims involved a tangible computer system, they did not reflect "an improvement in computers as tools".[41] The court thus held under *Alice* step two that the patent claims recited "nothing sufficient to remove [them] from the class of subject matter ineligible for patenting".[42] Simply limiting the claims to power grid monitoring, without anything more, was insufficient to transform the abstract idea into a patent-eligible concept.[43]

In *TDE Petroleum Data Solutions Inc v AKM Enterprise Inc*, the Federal Circuit similarly held ineligible claims directed to "various processes for determining the state of an oil well drill".[44] The claims in *TDE Petroleum* recited a method of receiving data from oil well sensors, validating the data by removing any erroneous data and determining the state of the oil well drill.[45] The court characterised the claims as "generally reciting 'collecting information, analyzing it, and displaying certain results of the collection and analysis'" and explained that that sort of "data gathering and processing claim" is directed to an abstract idea.[46] Under step two of the *Alice* test, the court concluded that the claims did not add anything to the abstract idea of storing, gathering and analysing data.[47] The court also noted that, although the patent specification disclosed embodiments for the step of applying the analysis to "automatically select ... one of the states [of the drill] as the state of the well operation", the claims did not recite any of those details.[48] The court, therefore, held the claims patent ineligible.[49]

The US District Court for the District of Maryland rejected claims directed to electric vehicle (EV) charging stations connected to a remote server via a network, where the remote server stores a variety of information.[50] The claims allegedly provided improvements to existing technology by creating a customised user experience and managing electric flow based on electric grid data by "filling the need for an 'efficient communication network' between charging stations, customers, and electric utility companies".[51] The district court nonetheless held the claims patent ineligible.[52] With respect to *Alice* step one, the district court found that the claims were directed to the abstract idea of "sending a request, receiving a command, and executing the command over a network".[53] With respect to *Alice* step two, the court found that the claims failed to transform that abstract idea into a patent-eligible inventive concept.[54] The district court noted that the claims "merely recite[d] the process of sending a request to a server and receiving back a command which is executed in a known way" or simply "narrow[ed] the known concept of responding to a demand response system in a particular field, in this case EV charging".[55]

Although many energy industry patents claiming digital technologies are invalidated under §101, a few cases provide clues about how to survive §101 challenges. In *Canrig Drilling Technology Ltd v Trinidad Drilling LP*, for example, the US District Court for the Southern District of Texas analysed claims "directed to a physical apparatus and drilling process of controlled rotation by a specific amount (the predetermined angle)".[56] The court rejected the argument that the claims were "directed to" the abstract idea of rotation.[57] The court explained that the claims addressed "specific challenges in directional drilling through a concrete process for controlling the rotation of the long drill strings to and between predetermined angles".[58] It reasoned that, although "rotation in isolation is an abstract concept" the claimed process "uses controlled rotation with predetermined angles to orient and oscillate a drill string", which improved on prior art processes.[59] The court thus concluded that the claimed invention provided a tangible improvement to the prior method of direct drilling and was not ineligible under §101.[60]

The Federal Circuit applied similar reasoning in *Thales Visionix Inc v United States*, a case that involved a patent claiming systems for tracking the motion of an object relative to a moving reference frame.[61] Inertial sensors can be used in aircraft navigation systems, calculating the position, orientation and velocity of an aircraft in three-dimensional space without the need for external information.[62] The Federal Circuit rejected the idea that the claimed systems were "directed to" using mathematical equations to determine the relative position of a moving object.[63] Instead, the court explained that the systems applied those mathematical equations to use inertial sensors in a non-conventional manner, improving the performance of the system relative to the prior art.[64] The court thus held that the claims were not "directed to" an abstract idea and were patent eligible under §101.[65]

These recent patent-eligibility decisions not only show how challenging it can be to overcome §101 challenges, but they also provide guidance on how to draft patent claims to have the best chance to survive such challenges. Many of the claims held ineligible involved collecting and analysing information, often without requiring any tangible action as a result of the analysis. In *TDE Petroleum*, for example, the Federal Circuit held the claims ineligible because they recited no more than storing, gathering and analysing data. Many of the cases where claims were upheld, on the other hand, used underlying information and analysis to perform some concrete steps. The claims in *Canrig*, for example, did more than analyse information about a drill string – they also extended to controlling the drill string based on the analysis. The claimed methods and systems allowed directional drilling by rotating a drill string to a predetermined angle and reducing friction by oscillating the drill string between predetermined angles.

Applying the lessons from these cases, companies should draft patent claims to recite a *practical application* of any underlying abstract idea, ideally tying any underlying concept or data gathering steps to a physical activity or the equipment from which data is being gathered.

Another common feature of patents that survive patent-eligibility challenges is that they clearly set out how the claims improve over the prior art and how they operate in ways that are not merely conventional. In *Thales*, for example, the Federal Circuit noted that the claims reflected an unconventional configuration of inertial sensors and choice of the reference frame against which position was measured. Companies, therefore, should draft patents with sufficient detail about how their invention improves on the prior art and how the patent claims "transform" any underlying abstract idea. This is particularly critical for patents involving digital technology and

AI, which are more likely to be challenged as reciting mere information gathering/analysis and as not reflecting any practical application of that analysis. Patents should include a description of how the claims improve the underlying system, whether that is the AI itself, the computer system running the AI or a physical system in the real world (eg, a drill string or power grid). Patents should also include sufficient description of any unconventional elements that the claims recite and tie those elements to how the claims improve on the prior art. Most cases where the patentee loses on *Alice* step two involve patents that failed to include such disclosure. A company can maximise its chances of success by providing adequate disclosure in its patent specifications about how its invention applies any underlying ideas and about the unconventional aspects that improve on the prior art.

3.2 Strategies for avoiding inventorship issues

When it comes to patents based on AI, companies must think strategically about inventorship issues, whether they are seeking to obtain an AI patent or are facing one in litigation. When prosecuting a patent covering an AI-based invention, companies should draft claims to focus on inventive aspects conceived by humans. This can decrease the chances of a challenge that the named human inventors did not conceive the full scope of the invention. Additionally, claiming

"When it comes to patents based on AI, companies must think strategically about inventorship issues, whether they are seeking to obtain an AI patent or are facing one in litigation."

inventive aspects that were created entirely by AI risks challenges based on the sufficiency of the patent's disclosure, including that the human inventor did not possess the full scope of the invention at the time of filing and that a skilled artisan would need to engage in undue experimentation to practice the aspects performed by the AI system.

Companies facing an AI-based patent in litigation should consider exactly these kinds of arguments to challenge the patents being asserted against them. For example, they should determine if there is a potential inventorship challenge because the named human inventors did not conceive of the full scope of the claimed inventions. And to the extent that a patent claim recites elements contributed by both humans and an AI system, develop written description, enablement and obviousness challenges to the aspects contributed by the AI system.

4. Trade secrets: strategies for navigating common pitfalls

A trade secret can potentially protect a broader group of competitive assets than patents and is better suited to protecting certain types of technology. For example, it is often challenging to assert patent claims covering chemical processes because competitors typically do not publicly disclose the parameters of their processes, which are performed behind closed doors. Thus, a trade secret on chemical process technology can be a smart strategic choice. Trade secrets similarly can be the most effective form of protection for innovations based on data analysis – including AI and digital technology – which, as discussed above, are sometimes difficult to patent.

In view of the challenges described above, what should companies do to ensure they adequately protect their trade secrets on AI and digital technologies?

First, they must ensure they understand the full scope of the information they possess that constitutes a trade secret. This could include not only scientific and technical know-how but also innovations relating to subsurface data, manufacturing techniques, computer algorithms and any other information that is secret and has commercial value. Companies often fail to appreciate the breadth of the information that trade secrets can protect, and thus fail to protect the full scope of their trade secrets. Companies should also identify and log trade secrets so they can later establish that they had already identified the information as a trade secret and treated it as such.

Companies must also ensure they take reasonable measures to maintain the secrecy of their trade secrets. The question of what secrecy measures will be viewed as 'reasonable' depends on the information being protected and the company's circumstances. But, there are many baseline secrecy measures companies can take. Perhaps most importantly, they should limit access to trade secrets to those employees and business partners who *absolutely* need to know them. Companies should secure physical facilities so only authorised people have access to trade secret information and limit access to electronic data to authorised users. They should also implement IT measures to protect secrecy, including:

- using password security for all files and additional security for trade secret information;
- limiting employees' ability to save files on local or portable drives;
- preventing employees from accessing company files via public or non-secure networks;
- requiring employees to return all laptops and external drives when they leave the company; and
- preventing employees from downloading, copying or deleting any data or files.

When considering what secrecy measures are required, companies should remember that former employees pose the greatest potential threat to trade secret misappropriation.[66] A few recent cases illustrate the risk posed by a company's own employees, who often have access to trade secret information and later leave (or are recruited) to work for a competitor. In a 2018 case, Sinovel, a Chinese manufacturer and exporter of wind turbines, was found guilty of misappropriating trade secrets from American Superconductor Corp (AMSC).[67] The trade secrets protected software used to regulate the flow of electricity from wind turbines to electrical grids. According to an affidavit submitted by an FBI agent,[68] Sinovel recruited an AMSC engineer, who unlawfully downloaded source code for the trade secret software from an AMSC server and provided a modified version to Sinovel. Total IP revenue losses from the trade secret theft were alleged to be approximately US$445 million.[69] Ultimately, Sinovel was fined US$1.5 million and agreed to pay more than US$58 million in restitution.[70] The engineer was placed on probation for one year.[71]

Similarly, Clean Energy filed a suit against Trillium Transportation Fuels LLC and Trillium USA Co alleging misappropriation of trade secrets, including confidential information about Clean Energy's customers, pricing and marketing strategies.[72] Clean Energy argued that a former employee who left to work with direct competitor Trillium took trade secrets with him and then recruited another Clean Energy employee, who took additional trade secret information with him. The second employee allegedly used a personal USB drive to download hundreds of confidential files the day before he resigned from Clean Energy.

The same risks that arise when employees leave a company similarly apply when dealing with third parties. In one recent case, GE alleged misappropriation of trade secret gas turbine technology by Siemens Energy Inc.[73] GE asserted that, while bidding against Siemens on a project for Dominion Energy Inc, GE provided Dominion with confidential trade secrets about GE's turbine manufacturing. According to GE, a Dominion employee shared GE's trade secrets with a Siemens sales manager on multiple occasions. GE alleged that, rather than destroy the trade secret information after receipt, the Siemens employee disseminated them to dozens of other employees using his Siemens email address.

Given the risks posed by employees and business partners, companies must ensure their employment agreements and third-party contracts adequately protect trade secrets. In fact, the sufficiency of a company's confidentiality agreements is a factor that courts consider in evaluating the reasonableness of the company's secrecy measures. Companies should require employees and outside parties alike to sign agreements acknowledging both that they have access to the trade secrets and that they have an ongoing obligation to maintain confidentiality. Companies should reinforce the ongoing nature of the confidentiality obligation in exit interviews for departing

"When considering what secrecy measures are required, companies should remember that former employees pose the greatest potential threat to trade secret misappropriation."

employees. In the case of third parties, the agreement should also impose certain minimum standards that the third party will use to protect the trade secret information.

Companies should be particularly careful to protect trade secrets when they enter into collaborations with other companies, who may be industry competitors. Joint ventures and other collaborations typically involve sharing information that might otherwise be closely guarded. Companies should avoid sharing trade secrets or other confidential know-how unless necessary and they should ensure their partner adequately protects the confidential information they receive. For example, joint venture agreements or other collaboration agreements should detail trade secret ownership, acknowledge the value of the trade secrets being shared, and set out detailed secrecy measures that all parties must employ to protect the information. The secrecy measures a company requires of its business partners is another factor courts consider when determining whether a trade secret owner used reasonable measures to protect its information. Collaboration agreements should also set out a protocol for the return or destruction of trade secret information upon termination of the collaboration.

"Digitalisation and AI will be increasingly important in the energy sector over the coming years, and these technologies will impact every aspect of the industry."

In addition to maintaining proper confidentiality in a joint venture, companies should also maintain strong, internal trade secret policies. Such policies should, for example, describe processes for identifying trade secrets and set out the required secrecy measures, including who has access and how decisions are made regarding the sharing of information. It is also important to ensure the policies are applied uniformly across a company's different business segments. For example, the R&D and commercial teams should both have the same understanding of who can disclose certain trade secret information and when. Strong internal policies are the base for strong joint venture policies.

Finally, companies should exercise caution when they possess trade secrets or other know-how in areas that are likely to be subject to regulatory scrutiny. Increased government regulation in the energy industry has created challenges for companies in protecting their trade secrets, such as when the government seeks disclosure of proprietary information for safety or environmental compliance reasons. For example, in response to public and governmental pressure, Baker Hughes stated that it would publicly disclose a complete list of the products and chemical ingredients used in its hydraulic fracturing fluid.[74] Although Baker Hughes declined to disclose the specific formulations of its fracking fluids, which were protected by trade secrets, it nonetheless disclosed more than other companies have chosen to divulge.

5. Conclusion

Digitalisation and AI will be increasingly important in the energy sector over the coming years, and these technologies will impact every aspect of the industry. Even companies that traditionally avoided the IP issues involved in digitalisation and AI can no longer look the other way. Despite the wide range of potential issues, addressing these issues proactively will help companies leverage the full scope of available IP protection, including patents and trade secrets, to protect and commercialise their investment in digitalisation and AI innovations. The fourth industrial revolution is here, and the companies that are most successful at developing, protecting and implementing digital innovations will lead the way.

Notes

1 Hannah Ritchie and Max Roser, "Energy Production and Consumption" (2020), https://ourworldindata.org/energy-production-consumption.
2 *Ibid.*
3 International Energy Agency (IEA), "Digitalization & Energy" (2017), https://iea.blob.core.windows.net/assets/b1e6600c-4e40-4d9c-809d-1d1724c763d5/DigitalizationandEnergy3.pdf.
4 *Ibid.*
5 Eka Software Solutions, "The Benefits of Artificial Intelligence for Energy Companies" (3 November 2021), www.altenergymag.com/article/2021/03/the-benefits-of-artificial-intelligence-for-energy-companies/34656.

6 Bernard Marr, "The Incredible Ways Shell Uses Artificial Intelligence to Help Transform the Oil and Gas Giant" (2019), www.forbes.com/sites/bernardmarr/2019/01/18/the-incredible-ways-shell-uses-artificial-intelligence-to-help-transform-the-oil-and-gas-giant/#76bd75d62701.
7 Christopher Helman, "How Algorithms Are Taking Over Big Oil" (2019), www.forbes.com/sites/christopherhelman/2019/01/14/how-algorithms-are-taking-over-big-oil/#679268808e2f.
8 General Electric (GE) press release, "GE Integrating AI to Enable Performance-Informed Gas Turbine Inverse Design" (24 June 2020), www.ge.com/news/press-releases/ge-integrating-ai-enable-performance-informed-gas-turbine-inverse-design-0.
9 Nicholas Nhede, "Excel and Partners Leverage AI to Transform Grid Asset Management" (31 January 2020), www.smart-energy.com/industry-sectors/energy-grid-management/excel-energy-and-partners-leverage-ai-to-transform-grid-asset-management/.
10 The SunShot Initiative was launched by the US Department of Energy on 4 February 2011, aiming to reduce the total costs of solar energy by 75%. See US Department of Energy – Office of Energy Efficiency & Renewable Energy, "The Sunshot Initiative", www.energy.gov/eere/solar/sunshot-initiative.
11 Thierry Mortier, "Why Artificial Intelligence Is a Game Changer for Renewable Energy" (24 November 2020), www.ey.com/en_us/power-utilities/why-artificial-intelligence-is-a-game-changer-for-renewable-energy.
12 *Ibid.*
13 World Economic Forum, "White Paper: Digital Transformation Initiative – Oil and Gas Industry" (January 2017), http://reports.weforum.org/digital-transformation/wp-content/blogs.dir/94/mp/files/pages/files/dti-oil-and-gas-industry-white-paper.pdf.
14 Harsh Choudhry, Azam Mohammad, Khoon Tee Tan and Richard Ward, "The Next Frontier for Digital Technologies in Oil and Gas" (25 August 2016), www.mckinsey.com/industries/oil-and-gas/our-insights/the-next-frontier-for-digital-technologies-in-oil-and-gas.
15 See n 3.
16 *Ibid.*
17 *Ibid.*
18 *Ibid.*
19 *Alice Corp Pty Ltd v CLS Bank International*, 573 US 208, 217 (2014).
20 *Electric Power Group LLC v Alstom SA*, 830 F.3d 1350 (Fed. Cir. 2016).
21 www.uspto.gov/sites/default/files/documents/16524350_22apr2020.pdf.
22 *Ibid.*
23 European Patent Office (EPO), "Artificial Intelligence" (4 November 2021), www.epo.org/news-events/in-focus/ict/artificial-intelligence.html.
24 www.ipo.gov.uk/p-challenge-decision-results/o74119.pdf.
25 *Ibid.* See also https://register.epo.org/application?documentId=E4B63SD62191498&number=EP18275163; https://register.epo.org/application?documentId=E4B63OBI2076498&number=EP18275174.
26 IPWatchdog, "DABUS Gets Its First Patent in South Africa Under Formalities Examination" (29 July 2021), www.ipwatchdog.com/2021/07/29/dabus-gets-first-patent-south-africa-formalities-examination/id=136116/.
27 United States Patent and Trademark Office (USPTO), "Public Views on Artificial Intelligence and Intellectual Property Policy" (October 2020), www.uspto.gov/sites/default/files/documents/USPTO_AI-Report_2020-10-07.pdf.
28 *Ibid.*
29 Korean Intellectual Property Office (KIPO), "Heads of KIPO and USPTO Agree on Reinforcing Cooperative Efforts on AI-related Policies" (23 October 2020), www.kipo.go.kr/en/BoardApp/UEngBodApp?c=1003&board_id=kiponews&catmenu=ek06_01_01&seq=1699.
30 Xiaoming Zhang, "China Set to Introduce Further Protection for AI-related Innovations" (7 January 2021), www.managingip.com/article/b1q04rqqg7tm9s/china-set-to-introduce-further-protection-for-ai-related-innovations.
31 Japan Patent Office (JPO), "Recent Trends in AI-related Inventions – Report" (August 2021), www.jpo.go.jp/e/system/patent/gaiyo/ai/document/ai_shutsugan_chosa/report.pdf.
32 WIPO Technology Trends, "Artificial Intelligence" (2019), www.wipo.int/edocs/pubdocs/en/wipo_pub_1055.pdf.
33 *Ibid.*
34 *Ibid.*
35 *Ibid.*
36 See 18 USC §1839(3).
37 *Alice Corp Pty Ltd v CLS Bank International*, 573 US 208, 217 (2014); *Mayo Collaborative Servs v Prometheus Labs Inc*, 566 US 66, 73 (2012).
38 573 US 208 at 223–224 (2014).
39 *Electric Power Group LLC v Alstom SA*, 830 F.3d 1350 at 1351 (Fed. Cir. 2016).
40 *Ibid.* at 1353.
41 *Ibid.* at 1354.
42 *Ibid.*
43 *Ibid.* at 1354–1355.
44 *TDE Petroleum Data Solutions Inc v AKM Enterprise Inc*, 657 Fed. App'x 991, 992 (Fed. Cir. 2016).

45 *Ibid.*
46 *Ibid.* at 993.
47 *Ibid.*
48 *Ibid.*
49 *Ibid.*
50 *ChargePoint Inc v SemaConnect Inc*, 2018 WL 1471685, *1–*2 (D. Md. 23 March 2018).
51 *Ibid.* at *1.
52 *Ibid.* at *5–*23.
53 The abstract idea was slightly different for some claims, but the concept was generally the same. See, eg, *ibid.* at *8.
54 *Ibid.* at *17–*23.
55 *Ibid.*
56 *Canrig Drilling Technology Ltd v Trinidad Drilling LP*, 2015 WL 5458576, *4 (S.D. Tex. Sept. 17, 2015).
57 *Ibid.*
58 *Ibid.*
59 *Ibid.*
60 *Ibid.*
61 *Thales Visionix Inc v United States*, 850 F.3d 1343, 1345 (Fed. Cir. 2017).
62 *Ibid.* at 1344–1345.
63 *Ibid.* at 1348.
64 *Ibid.* at 1348–1349.
65 *Ibid.* at 1349.
66 American Society of Industrial Security (ASIS), "Trends in Proprietary Information Loss Survey Report" (September 2002), p8, Table 3.1, www.diogenesllc.com/trendsproprietaryloss.pdf.
67 United States Department of Justice (US DOJ) press release, "Chinese Company Sinovel Wind Group Convicted of Theft of Trade Secrets" (24 January 2018), www.justice.gov/opa/pr/chinese-company-sinovel-wind-group-convicted-theft-trade-secrets.
68 Before the Defend Trade Secrets Act was enacted in 2016, claims of trade secret misappropriation at the US federal level were governed by the Economic Espionage Act of 1996 and prosecuted by the US DOJ rather than by private litigants.
69 See *United States v Sinovel Wind Group Co*, No 3:13-cr-00084-JDP (D. Wisc. 9 July 2018), ECF No 498.
70 See *United States v Sinovel Wind Group Co*, No 3:13-cr-00084-JDP (D. Wisc. 10 July 2018), ECF No 499.
71 *Ibid.*
72 See *Clean Energy v Trillium Transportation Fuels LLC*, No 19-cv-00244 (S.D. Tex. Dec. 13, 2018), ECF No 1.
73 *General Electric Co v Siemens Energy Inc*, Complaint & Demand for Jury Trial, No 21-cv-00025 (E.D. Va. 14 Jan. 2021), ECF No 1.
74 Kevin Bagos and Matthew Daly, "Major Oil, Gas Firm to List Fracking Chemicals" (24 April 2014), www.usatoday.com/story/money/business/2014/04/24/major-oil-and-gas-firm-to-list-fracking-chemicals/8122885.

"Standards are everywhere in the energy industry. Gas, oil and electricity standards are ubiquitous and critical for public and consumer safety and to ensure continuous supplies."

V. Standard essential patents: licensing challenges for energy companies

Robert Pocknell
Keystone Law

As companies in the energy industry make use of the Internet of Things (IoT) and communication technology in products and services, some telecommunications (telecoms) companies have decided that they want a share of the resulting revenue and are seeking patent licences from energy companies that are selling connected devices and services.

A few patent holders are seeking to create a revenue stream from the licensing of end devices on the basis of the device price, and they do this by refusing to grant patent licences to certain suppliers of telecoms equipment further down the supply chain or by extracting excessive royalties. The refusal to grant licences means that some equipment suppliers cannot pass the necessary intellectual property (IP) rights up the supply chain to their customers, and this means that end devices are not licensed when they are sold or used, and so the patent holders can threaten energy companies with injunctions unless they pay the excessive royalty fees demanded.

In this chapter, we will explore some of the patent licensing issues that the energy industry needs to consider in the era of climate change and sustainability, as well as the use of wireless functionality and other common standards. IP practitioners in the energy industry should make themselves aware of these issues – both in the context of supply contracts and their risk management, as well as managing the risk of claims under warranties and indemnities in mergers and acquisitions – given the potential for historical claims.

1. Standards in the energy industry

Standards are everywhere in the energy industry. Gas, oil and electricity standards are ubiquitous and critical for public and consumer safety and to ensure continuous supplies. Standards in the energy industry have been developed over the years by the British Standards Institution (BSI), the German Institute for Standardisation (DIN) and many other national standards organisations. As we have moved into a connected world, a raft of new standards have been, and are being, developed and used that will need to be understood by the energy industry. Here are just a few examples:

1.1 Smart meters

Smart meter systems use Wide Area Networks (WAN) and Home Areas Networks (HAN). A WAN is a network which allows smart meters to connect to servers of energy supply companies. A HAN is a secure network that links smart devices within homes.

On 14 May 2021, the Data Communications Company (DCC), which was set up by the UK government to manage smart meter

"As we have moved into a connected world, a raft of new standards have been, and are being, developed and used that will need to be understood by the energy industry."

communications through a secure network to energy suppliers, reported that the amount of 'live' smart meters was 11,811,493.

The global smart meter market size was valued at US$21.13 billion in 2019 and is projected to reach US$39.20 billion by 2027, registering a compound annual growth rate (CAGR) of 8.80% during the forecast period.[1]

1.2 Autonomous driving

Standards in autonomous driving include BSI Guidance PAS 1880,[2] which provides a set of initial guidelines focused on developing safe control systems for automated vehicles (AVs). V2X is a vehicle communication system that incorporates other more specific types of communication such as V2I (vehicle-to-infrastructure), V2N (vehicle-to-network), V2V (vehicle to vehicle), V2P (vehicle-to-pedestrian), V2D (vehicle-to-device) and V2G (vehicle-to-grid).

The full economic value of the connected and autonomous vehicle (CAV) market could be worth £41.7 billion by 2035.[3] In January 2021, the UK Transport Minister, Rachel Maclean, said:

> *The investment in and development of CAVs could truly transform the way people and goods are transported, with innovation like this at the heart of our ambition to build back better. We're on the cusp of a driving revolution. Not only could this tech unlock vast opportunities for the UK economy and jobs market, it could significantly improve the safety and efficiency of how we travel over the coming decades.*[4]

1.3 Electric vehicle charging

Electric vehicle (EV) charge points are used to provide charging to EV's with a battery and the electrical source that helps to charge the battery. Different standards in EV charging have been developed, including CHADeMO (an IEEE standard), CCS (Combined Charging System) and Tesla proprietary standards.

There are a number of companies that are looking to charge licence fees for companies using the standard.[5]

The EV charger market size was valued at US$3.8 billion in 2019 and is projected to reach US$25.5 billion by 2027, registering a CAGR of 26.8% from 2020 to 2027.[6]

2. What is the standards-setting process?

Standards are usually developed by standards setting organisations (SSOs). SSOs include international organisations such as the European Telecommunications Standards Institute (ETSI) and the Institute of

Electrical and Electronics Engineers (IEEE), but also national organisations such as the BSI and DIN. Typically, industry representatives and other interested parties meet in SSO working groups to discuss the technological solutions to incorporate in a particular standard. During that process, representatives may make proposals to include technology in the standard; the proposed technology may be covered by a patent or pending patent application held by the representative's company. If the proposed technology is adopted into the standard and it is covered by a patent, that patent is said to be 'essential to using the standard'. A patent that must be infringed when a product uses the standard is generally called a 'standard essential patent' (SEP).

In the normal course of things, if a patent is infringed by someone using the standard and is otherwise valid and enforceable, the patent owner can require the sellers and users of products infringing the patent to stop making and using the products. To avoid a SEP owner unfairly exploiting this leverage to demand supra-competitive royalties or to exclude standards-compliant products from the market, many SSOs require the owner of a SEP to voluntarily commit to license SEPs on fair, reasonable and non-discriminatory (FRAND) terms to third parties (this might also be royalty-free licensing, such as, Bluetooth, for example). This FRAND commitment is intended to be the cure for what would otherwise be an unlawful agreement among horizontal competitors to agree on a single standardised set of technical solutions, rather than compete with one another on different technical solutions.

Despite that commitment, the meaning of FRAND is not defined, and this dynamic gives a SEP owner significant leverage over a potential licensee as it can threaten to obtain an injunction to prevent the sale of any product that uses the standard if the licensee will not agree to its licensing terms.

A company that has chosen to develop a product and use a standard in that product will have made significant investments in product design and production, all of which would be put at risk if it cannot use the standard.

While SSOs require participants to declare their SEPs to the SSO and voluntarily commit that they will license their SEPs on FRAND terms, SSOs do not have the resources to check whether companies comply with their commitments, or whether patents that are declared to be essential to a standard are actually essential (and also whether they are valid and otherwise enforceable, on which points only a court could make an authoritative determination).

"A company that has chosen to develop a product and use a standard in that product will have made significant investments in product design and production, all of which would be put at risk if it cannot use the standard."

Many SSO policies require disclosure of patents or patent applications before a standard is set. Moreover, the requirements and policies are not uniform, and in many SSOs the system is opaque and confusing, particularly to those not familiar with the technology in the standard.

3. What SEP issues arise in the standards-setting process?
Over the years the telecoms industry has seen many examples of different issues that make the licensing environment complex and difficult for new entrants, stakeholders and courts to understand and grapple with.

In addition, participants in the standards-setting process have many different strategies, including:

- inflating the size of their portfolios by filing multiple patents relating to optional or minor incremental features;
- where there may be a choice between several options of equal use to the standard, pushing for features that read on a participant's patent;
- holding back the disclosure of patents until after the standard has been set;
- filing patent applications for inventions that, in fact, are neither novel nor inventive; and

- filing patent applications while the standard is being discussed and based on the ideas of other participants.

SSOs and participants come up with new versions of standards, which are often small increments in the standardisation process, and which reuse a lot of technology and ideas from earlier versions of the standards. The strategy of many companies is to always push for a new standard which needs to be licensed, and for which SEP holders can seek to charge higher fees.

As it transpires, in practice most SEPs that have been declared 'essential' are more than likely not actually essential. According to a number of studies, 70% to 90% of alleged SEPs, when tested in court, are found either non-essential, invalid or not infringed. Indeed, only a tiny fraction (about 6%) of SEP-related court cases brought by non-practising entities (companies that do not actually sell products implementing standards, but merely hold SEPs) are successful in establishing essentiality, validity and/or infringement.

Because there are tens of thousands of patents that are declared essential to, for example, the 5G standard (in part due to over-declaration of SEPs), it is prohibitively costly – particularly for small and medium-sized enterprises (SMEs) and new entrants to the field – to navigate the thicket of declared SEPs.

The standards-setting process is, therefore, fraught with issues, and then finally, when the standard has been adopted, there will be a number of companies that own SEPs, and some will seek to license them. Under the IP rights policy of many SSOs, the SEPs must be licensed on FRAND terms, and that is when a new set of issues emerges.

4. What does FRAND (fair, reasonable and non-discriminatory) mean?

We know what the acronym stands for, and it is easy for companies to say they will license SEPs on FRAND terms. However, in practice, billions of pounds have been, and are being, spent on litigation between companies that cannot agree on what FRAND means and how much should be paid to whom, and by whom, in the supply chain.

Some of the arguments that come up in the FRAND debate in the telecoms industry include:

- What is a fair licensing rate? (ie, what does the 'F' in FRAND mean?)
- What is a reasonable licensing rate? (ie, what does the 'R' in FRAND mean?)

- What does non-discriminatory mean? (ie, what does the 'ND' in FRAND mean?)
- Can SEP holders charge different SEP rates to SMEs compared to multinationals?
- Should there be a public price list?
- Should there be one price for SEPs for all implementers of the standard?
- Should the licensing fees and rates that SEP owners charge be publicly available, given that the standard is public?
- Should the SEP be valued on the component that uses the standard and infringes the patent?
- Should the SEP be valued on the price of the end device or the component that uses the standard and infringes the patent?
- Should the value of the SEP be based on the value of the patent to the standard?
- What is a reasonable royalty rate for all SEPs for each standard?
- Should there be a cumulative royalty cap, or fixed price, for all royalties for all SEPs in a standard?
- Should the royalty (and/or royalty cap) be fixed and published before the standard is set (*ex ante*)?
- What is a reasonable per patent rate?
- Is the use of the SEP optional or mandatory?
- How many SEPs are there for the whole of the standard?
- What share of all SEPs does each SEP holder have?
- Should every company in the supply chain be able to get a SEP licence on FRAND terms?
- Can SEP holders selectively refuse to license some companies in the supply chain?
- Can SEP owners 'turn a blind eye' to infringement by some companies, and yet sue others?
- Is there any agreement among SEP owners about the pricing of SEPs?
- Does the FRAND encumbrance travel with the patent, for example, if it is assigned to another company?
- How does a transfer of a patent (or group of patents) affect the value of the remaining portfolio?
- Does a single patent transferred from a portfolio of patents to another company mean that a single patent is worth more outside of the portfolio?
- Should there be injunctions for SEPs?
- Should there be injunctions for critical sectors (eg, eCall for cars or safety-critical industries like gas or electricity installations)?
- Should a court in one country be able to set a global rate for a SEP or a portfolio of SEPs?

As you might imagine, there are many divergent views between: (1) companies claiming to own SEPs; (2) those companies from whom they demand licensing fees; and (3) those companies that are refused licences by SEP holders.

For those companies from whom they demand royalties, SEP owners threaten them with injunctions unless they pay the rates demanded (whether or not they are FRAND). Several SEP owners also demand that the royalties be based on the use to which the standard is put.

SEP owners are unwilling to give warranties that their SEPs are licensed on FRAND terms and often hide behind non-disclosure agreements, charging hugely varying rates to different types of companies, depending on their size. SEP holders often make representations about licensing terms which they are unwilling to put in writing in an agreement.

Some SEP owners say that they do not have to grant licences to any company that wants one and that they can decide who in the supply chain they want to grant licences to. Companies that want a licence have complained to competition authorities. In 2020, the question of whether Nokia could refuse to license suppliers to Daimler was going to be considered by the European Court of Justice (ECJ), following a referral by the German courts, but Nokia settled their case with

"As with most industries, the energy industry has a long history of dealings in the supply chain where sellers of components give warranties and indemnities to their customers."

Daimler, and so the referral to the ECJ fell away. In the US, Continental, which is a supplier to Daimler, is seeking an order that Nokia grant licences to its suppliers. The Directorate General for Competition at the European Commission is still considering the issue.

In the UK, the Competition and Markets Authority (CMA) issued guidance in January 2021 in relation to sustainability agreements as follows:[7]

> *Many sustainability agreements are standard-setting agreements by which businesses, often through trade associations or standardisation organisations, set standards on the environmental performance of products, production processes, or the resources used in production.*
>
> *When setting up a new standard, businesses, trade associations and/or standardisation organisations should ... ensure access to the standard is on fair, reasonable and non-discriminatory terms for all businesses which comply with it ... [and] must also offer to license their essential IPR to all third parties on fair, reasonable and non-discriminatory terms.*

It remains to be seen whether the CMA takes any action against companies refusing to grant licences to SEPs to those companies that want one.

These are just a few of the issues that SEP owners, potential licensees, courts, legislators and competition authorities have to grapple with.

5. Why are these telecoms issues relevant to the energy industry?

As with most industries, the energy industry has a long history of dealings in the supply chain where sellers of components give warranties and indemnities to their customers. These buyers rely on the warranties and indemnities they are given and assume that the seller has obtained the necessary IP rights. The risk profile of the supply chain is generally understood by those in it, and the purchasing and sales departments can assess and manage risk.

If some SEP holders, as indicated above, refuse to grant licences to all companies in the supply chain, this leaves component vendors unable to supply products with the necessary patent rights, and that means customers and end users are potentially liable for infringement risks.

All of this creates uncertainty and complexity in the supply chain of the energy industry.

5.1 Example: a 'smart' water flow meter

An example of this might involve a standard (non-cellular) water flow meter. Assume the manufacturer of the meter designs it, buys the components and manufactures it and then sells it to an energy company. The energy company seeks IP warranties and indemnities (that the manufacturer can pass on all of the necessary IP rights) and assesses the creditworthiness of the manufacturer, the limitations of liability and manages the risk. The energy company will expect the manufacturer to have the necessary IP rights.

Let us assume in the example that the energy company says it wants a 'smart' water flow meter so it can access information and data remotely, thereby improving the service to its customers.

A typical supply chain for a smart gas meter might have four or five (or more) participants in the chain buying and selling products, such as:

- the Wi-Fi chip supplier (the chip with the Wi-Fi functionality that meets the Wi-Fi standard);
- the module supplier (incorporating the Wi-Fi chip);
- the smart meter manufacturer (incorporating the module);
- the distributor (buying from the smart meter manufacturer and selling to the energy utility company); and
- the utility company (buying the smart meter and selling it to end users).

The manufacturer agrees to invest in the innovation and design of a new smart water meter with Wi-Fi capability. The Wi-Fi capability is derived from a chipset, and the chipset will infringe the SEP. The chipset is made by a chipset supplier (Supplier 1), who will sell it to a module manufacturer (Supplier 2) for incorporation into a Wi-Fi communications module. The manufacturer goes to the Wi-Fi module supplier (Supplier 2) to buy the communications module.

If the Wi-Fi owner refuses to grant SEP licences to Supplier 1, Supplier 1 will not be able to sell the product to the module manufacturer (Supplier 2) with all the necessary IP rights, and it will be selling products which potentially infringe the rights of the SEP owner.

If the Wi-Fi owner refuses to grant SEP licences to Supplier 1 or Supplier 2, Supplier 2 will not be able to sell the product to the smart water flow meter manufacturer with all the necessary IP rights, and it will be selling products potentially infringing the rights of the SEP owner.

The manufacturer cannot, therefore, obtain the necessary IP rights

"Remember that the SEP infringement is not about infringing the patent 'in a smart meter', but about infringing the SEP when making a Wi-Fi standard compliant product."

from its supplier and is left with claims made against it under the warranty and indemnity provisions in the supply contract with its utility company customer, as well as being itself exposed to claims from SEP holders that it is infringing the Wi-Fi SEPs. The manufacturer could seek licences to the SEPs, but it does not know if it will be able to get SEP licences or who to obtain them from and, even if it did, it would be faced with dealing with claims concerning technology it is not familiar with. The manufacturer will have limited knowledge of how the Wi-Fi module works, and/or whether the patents are valid or infringed or what the real FRAND rate is.

In addition, SEP holders will claim royalties for all devices that a company uses or sells, not only in the future, but also in the last six years. Therefore, all companies in the supply chain will need to take into account past sales.

If we assume there is a valid SEP that must be infringed when making a product compliant with the Wi-Fi standard, each of the participants in the supply chain can be infringing the SEP by using or selling a product that incorporates the Wi-Fi chip. Remember that the SEP infringement is not about infringing the patent 'in a smart meter', but about infringing the SEP when making a Wi-Fi standard compliant product.

Each of those five participants is exposed to risk in its buy/sell contracts in the supply chain. If the SEP holder refuses to grant a licence to the Wi-Fi chip supplier, it does not pass through the right to use the SEP to the module manufacturer and so on.

If the SEP holder refuses to grant licences to anyone in the supply chain except the utility company, then the SEP holder can threaten an injunction unless the utility company pays the royalty demanded by the SEP holder. For example, a company called Avanci[8] is the agent for a group of companies that claim to have the right to license about 50% of 3G and 4G SEPs. If Avanci was to claim a royalty of €5 per smart meter unit, a utility company may be threatened with a claim for €5 for all smart meters it has used and sold in the past six years which have 3G or 4G functionality, and that it sells in the future. In the UK alone, as previously mentioned at section 1.1, the number of 'live' smart meters on 14 May 2021 was 11,811,493, so claims for €5 per smart meter could run into the tens, if not hundreds, of millions of pounds and those costs will ultimately be passed on to the consumer.

For energy companies installing private networks, or 5G networks, for their facilities or for monitoring of their assets, it is imperative that they ensure that their suppliers have the necessary SEP licences and that their suppliers will be able to stand behind the warranties and indemnities they are providing for a minimum period of six years from the supply of the products or services.

For all suppliers, the current regime is a huge challenge because they will not want to give warranties and indemnities for amounts which could exceed the value of the product they are supplying. Even if they did give the warranties and indemnities, they may not have licences to all of the SEPs for the standards. Issues are made worse because many utility companies require a five-year fixed-price agreement so the risk needs to be reassessed, and contracts may need to be renegotiated.

6. What can be done?

For energy companies buying smart products, legal departments will need to educate and inform the finance and purchasing teams that they cannot just rely on common form indemnities and warranties from suppliers. For products that use standards, they will need to undertake a due diligence exercise to ascertain the IP rights that they do and do not have rights to, and they will need to assess, *inter alia*, the risk of direct claims being made by SEP holders, and the scope and financial viability of being able to make claims under warranties and indemnities from their suppliers. Where suppliers cannot provide evidence or assurances that they have the necessary SEP rights, they should consider engaging directly with the many companies claiming to have SEPs to explore the terms upon which

SEPs will be licensed to them. Consideration will also need to be given to the historic claims that may be made for past purchases and sales in the previous six years, and whether the warranties and indemnities are sufficient for the company's risk profile.

For suppliers of connected devices, they will need to talk to their own sub-suppliers about the warranties and indemnities that have been provided in their purchasing agreements. They will also need to undertake additional due diligence on the extent to which their suppliers have asked for SEP licences, what SEP licences they have and whether they have been refused licences. They should also consider engaging directly with companies claiming to have SEPs to explore the terms upon which SEPs will be licensed to them. They should also consider excluding SEPs from their warranties and indemnities and potentially seek to renegotiate existing contracts, given the likelihood of claims being made against their customers.

Suppliers and purchasers at all levels of the supply chain might want to talk to their industry organisations and ask them to speak to their governments and competition authorities in connection with the refusals to license.

Some further guidance and core principles and approaches for licensing of SEPs are available from CEN-CENELEC and DIN.[9]

Notes

1 Avinash Savekar and Vineet Kumar, "Smart Meter Market Outlook – 2030" (December 2021), www.alliedmarketresearch.com/smart-meters-market.
2 British Standards Institute (BSI), "PAS 1880:2020 Guidelines for Developing and Assessing Control Systems for Automated Vehicles", www.bsigroup.com/en-GB/CAV/pas-1880/.
3 UK Department of Transport, "UK on the Cusp of a Transport Revolution, as Self-Driving Vehicles Set to Be Worth Nearly £42 billion by 2035" (13 January 2021), www.gov.uk/government/news/uk-on-the-cusp-of-a-transport-revolution-as-self-driving-vehicles-set-to-be-worth-nearly-42-billion-by-2035.
4 Rachel Maclean, "2021 Comments on Self-Driving Cars" (14 January 2021), www.ukpol.co.uk/rachel-maclean-2021-comments-on-self-driving-cars/.
5 MPEG LA, "EV Charging", www.mpegla.com/programs/ev-charging/.
6 Akshay Jadhav and Veenit Kumar, "Electric Vehicle Charger Market Statistics – 2027" (April 2020), www.alliedmarketresearch.com/electric-vehicle-charger-evc-market.
7 UK Competition and Markets Authority (CMA), "Environmental Sustainability Agreements and Competition Law" (27 January 2021), www.gov.uk/government/publications/environmental-sustainability-agreements-and-competition-law.
8 See 'Smart Meters', www.avanci.com/vision/.
9 CEN-CENELEC and DIN, "Core Principles and Approaches for Licensing of Standard Essential Patents: CWA 95000" (June 2019), https://2020.standict.eu/sites/default/files/CWA95000.pdf.

"The value of a brand to a company in the energy sector must not be underestimated. Companies in the energy sector rely heavily on their brands to attract and retain customers."

VI. Brand protection

Sean Ibbetson
Bristows LLP

1. Introduction: the value of brands in the energy sector

The energy sector is not one which is most closely associated with highly valuable brands. In Forbes' latest ranking of the world's most valuable brands, there is not a single company from the energy sector in the top 100. However, this has not always been the case. Shell was on Forbes' list in 2015 and other traditional oil and gas giants have also had a recent presence. The absence today of the largest energy brands is likely due to the public's changing attitudes to traditional energy sources, and the fact that brands whose focus is on renewables have not yet gained the traction needed to take their place.

The value of a brand to a company in the energy sector must not, however, be underestimated. Companies in the energy sector rely heavily on their brands to attract and retain customers. Brands are also used to communicate to consumers that a particular product, or the company behind it, has certain characteristics or particular values.

This is critical in the energy sector for two main reasons.

First, consumers need reassurance that their energy products are genuine because this could have serious implications both in terms of performance and safety. Counterfeit fuel products pose a serious risk to both people and the vehicles or homes they are used in. The harm caused by a counterfeit fuel has potentially far worse consequences than a counterfeit t-shirt or wristwatch. Companies have and continue to seek innovative ways to confirm their product's authenticity to consumers and to dissuade counterfeiters. Examples include security markings, tags and even the shapes of containers. In each example, this mark of origin can be protected by intellectual property (IP) rights.

Secondly, the energy sector has increasingly been required to allay consumers' concerns with the harms which are caused or associated with traditional energy sources. Brands have increasingly sought to present themselves as being in transition away from high carbon emissions and towards lower carbon and renewable energy sources. It is more than 20 years since BP infamously rebranded itself as 'Beyond Petroleum'. Whilst that trademark remains registered by BP, the tagline is no longer prominently used. Nevertheless, BP recently committed itself to a similar vision, when it stated its ambition to pivot "from being an international oil company focused on producing resources to an integrated energy company focused on delivering solutions for customers".[1] Maintaining or establishing 'green' credentials has, therefore, become highly important and, again, brands are central to this effort.

In this chapter, we consider the legal issues associated with the protection of brands in the energy sector. We also cover the enforcement of those rights and consider the particular issues associated with the enforcement of rights in the context of online infringements.

2. How the energy sector protects its brands

This section examines: (1) what can be protected by trademarks, designs and copyright; (2) what scope of protection those rights afford their owner; and (3) how those in the energy sector have sought to protect their brands with these rights.

2.1 Trademarks (registered)

(a) Registrability issues

The purpose of a trademark is to designate, to consumers, the origin of a product or a service. In most circumstances, the most valuable tool in the protection of a brand is, therefore, a registered trademark.

The benefits of trademark registration are clear. A trademark can be secured relatively quickly and cheaply and, once registered, there is no limit on the length of time which a trademark can stay on the register (provided that: (1) the renewal fees are paid; (2) the trademark continues to be used; and (3) the trademark continues to be capable of operating as a trademark).

Most will be familiar with the registration of words and logos as registered trademarks. In certain jurisdictions, sounds, colours, shapes, patterns, motions and even holograms can also be registered.

There are basic requirements for registering a trademark which can present a challenge for energy sector brand owners just as they do in other industries, including that the sign chosen must be:

- **Distinctive:** this criteria is assessed by reference to the type of goods or services for which the trademark is registered. The word DIESEL, for example, can therefore operate as a trademark for clothing, but not for fuel products.
- **Clear and precise:** the chosen sign must be capable of being represented in a manner which enables the authorities and the public to determine the clear and precise subject matter of the protection afforded to the trademark's owner.

In the remainder of this section, we therefore consider the various types of trademark registrations which can be obtained, and look at how the energy sector has sought to use each category of trademark to protect its brand.

"There are basic requirements for registering a trademark which can present a challenge for energy sector brand owners just as they do in other industries."

(b) What types of signs have been registered as trademarks in the energy sector

Word marks: the most common – and often the most powerful – trademark rights are registered for the name of a company or its products.

A search of the UK's trademark identifies hundreds of word trademarks registered across each part of the energy sector, from some of the longest-trading entities to those who have only emerged in the last decade or so and who specialise in renewable energy.

Product names and associated services are often the subjects of registration too. BP, for example, owns multiple trademark registrations not just for its main brand (BP), but also for its engine lubricants (CASTROL) and its food and drinks offerings (WILD BEAN CAFÉ).

Logos: Logos are also registered. A logo can be registered without words or combined with words.

Companies who face difficulties registering word marks, perhaps because those words are descriptive or not sufficiently distinctive, often seek to secure protection by combining those words with a figurative mark. Parties taking this approach should, however, bear in mind the warning given by Mr Justice Arnold (as he then was) who famously warned that those who register descriptive trademarks "under the cover of a figurative fig leaf of distinctiveness" would likely face difficulties when it came to enforcing those trademarks against a party using the inherently unregistrable sign without the figurative element which enabled the trademark owner to secure registration.[2]

Logos provide an additional layer in a strategy to protect a brand, but when it comes to enforcement of trademark rights they almost always play a secondary role to word marks.

Logos are also updated periodically, as a brand's image evolves. A new logo or font might be adopted every few years in some cases. Trademark portfolios, therefore, need to be updated to reflect this, if logo registrations are to have any value.

Slogans: Slogans are also capable of registration. There are no additional legislative restrictions which apply specifically to slogans. However, the key requirements discussed at section 2.1(a) (namely that a trademark must be distinctive and not descriptive) are far more likely to catch a slogan than a more conventional word trademark.

Slogans are likely to be refused registration if they are phrases which

"Companies who face difficulties registering word marks, perhaps because those words are descriptive or not sufficiently distinctive, often seek to secure protection by combining those words with a figurative mark."

are commonly used, too simple, or laudatory. The UK Intellectual Property Office's (UKIPO) guidance gives "we lead the way" as an example of a slogan which is likely to be refused registration.

In the energy sector, there are many examples of slogans which have been registered. To take BP again as an example, a search of the UK register identifies a UK trademark for the words "PROTECTION FROM THE MOMENT",[3] which is used as part of the advertising slogan for Castrol.

As with logos, trademark litigation is not often pursued solely on the basis of a registered slogan trademark, but they nevertheless provide a valuable tool in brand protection, particularly where a tag line in an advertising campaign is used over many years and becomes central to a brand's identity.

Colour marks: many jurisdictions, including the UK and EU, provide for the registration of particular colours as trademarks.

The key obstacle, however, is likely to be proving that a colour is distinctive, in the sense that consumers will rely on it as indicating the origin of a product.

If that obstacle can be overcome, then the proprietor must also satisfy the registration requirements. In the UK, for example, an application to register a colour as a trademark must include a sample of the colour, a written description (eg, 'dark blue'), and a code from an internationally recognised colour identification system (such as Pantone).

Proprietors have also faced issues where the description implies (rather than defines categorically) how the colour will be used. In 2013, for example, the Court of Appeal held that Cadbury's trademark registration for the colour purple was invalid because it was described as being "applied to the whole visible surface, *or being the predominant colour* applied to the whole visible surface, of the packaging of the goods".[4] The Court of Appeal held that the use of the word "predominant" opened the door to a multitude of different visual forms, as it was unclear what other colours would be displayed on the packaging or how.

The energy sector has also been involved in the registration of colour trademarks. Both Shell and BP, for example, have multiple registrations which claim protection over colours or colour combinations. These include:

"It is difficult to assess, with any real certainty, how valuable any trademark is in the protection of a brand."

- BP's trademark registration No 00003393986 for a shade of green.
- Shell's trademark registration No 00917961558 for the combination of red and yellow.
- Shell's trademark registration No 00002310067 for the application of red and yellow to parts of vehicle service stations.

BP also owns a trademark protecting the combination of colours on a vehicle service station, and enforced this mark in trademark infringement proceedings involving a company that adopted green livery for its service stations in Northern Ireland.[5]

In that case, the Court of Appeal of Northern Ireland found in BP's favour – finding that there was a likelihood of confusion arising. The court was particularly persuaded by the argument that motorists who were travelling at speed might decide to turn off a road in the mistaken belief that the defendant's green petrol station was a BP petrol station. This type of initial confusion (ie, confusion which occurs but is then later dispelled before a purchase is made) gained some traction and was recognised as being actionable in a 2010 judgment of Mr Justice Arnold (as he then was) in *Och Ziff v OCH Capital*.[6] More recently, however, the Court of Appeal of England and Wales has cast doubt on whether such "initial interest confusion" is actionable.[7] There is, therefore, significant doubt as to whether BP would succeed again if it brought another claim on similar facts.

It is difficult to assess, with any real certainty, how valuable any trademark is in the protection of a brand. Colour marks are reasonably common. Many brands certainly like the idea of 'ownership' of a particular colour or shade of colour. However, as previously discussed, there are significant obstacles to successfully registering and enforcing colour trademarks. Despite this, they can provide a useful tool in efforts to stake a claim to a particular colour. And given the attractiveness of green, particularly to a brand in the energy sector, it is understandable that a company such as BP has been keen to claim exclusive rights in this way and why companies such as Shell have also sought protection for the use of their colours on premises such as service stations.

Shapes: the final major category of trademarks are shapes, which can be registered either with or without colour.

In the UK, legislation imposes additional restrictions on what can and cannot be registered as a shape mark meaning that a shape cannot be registered if it: (1) results from the nature of the goods themselves; (2) is necessary to obtain a technical result; or (3) gives substantial value to the goods.

Companies within the energy sector have been active in this field. By way of example, the UK trademark register contains shape marks which depict fuel tankers, gas canisters and packaging.

As with colour trademarks, proprietors can face difficulties when it comes to asserting shape marks. First, it is more likely that such marks will be challenged on the basis of distinctiveness and/or non-use, meaning that a claimant is put to the burden of proving its rights in order to get its claim off the ground. It can also be difficult to persuade a tribunal that consumers are likely to be confused when it comes to the infringement of a non-conventional mark, such as a registration for a shape or a colour, as – generally speaking – consumers are less accustomed to relying on shapes and colours as designators of the origin of a product.

We consider below the scope of protection which is afforded by registered trademarks.

(c) Infringement of a registered trademark

In summary, a registered trademark is infringed if a third party:

- Uses an identical sign (eg, BP or CASTROL) in relation to identical goods and services for which the trademark is registered (eg, fuels or lubricants). The typical application of this provision is in relation to counterfeit goods. Given that the infringement analysis is typically straightforward and difficult to dispute, allegations relating to counterfeit goods rarely reach the courts.
- Uses an identical sign in relation to similar goods or services, or a similar sign in relation to identical goods or services. In addition, the use of the sign must be likely to cause confusion on the part of the public. The typical application of this provision is where a third party's chosen brand is deemed too close to a competitor, such that consumers are likely to be confused into thinking they are the same product or are somehow related to each other. Evidence of actual confusion arising is not necessary, but it certainly helps a claimant. Conversely, if there have been many years of side-by-side trading and no evidence of confusion then the courts can be reluctant to hold that there is a likelihood of confusion arising in the future.
- Uses an identical or similar sign (on either similar or dissimilar goods/services), where the registered trademark has a reputation in the UK, and use of the sign is without due cause and either takes unfair advantage of, or is detrimental to, the distinctive character or the repute of the trademark. This provision widens the scope of protection for trademarks with a reputation – meaning that the trademark is known to a

significant part of the public concerned with the products and/or services covered. The trademark owner must then also prove that use of the sign will give rise to one or more of the following types of injury:

- **Unfair advantage:** for example, by the defendant engaging in some form of 'free-riding' on the back of the reputation of the trademark.
- **Detriment:** to either (1) the distinctive character or (2) the reputation of the trademark. Detriment to distinctive character is often described as a 'blurring' or 'dilution' of the trademark's distinctiveness. Detriment to reputation is often seen as activity which risks tarnishing the reputation of a trademark – perhaps by associating the trademark with a product of inferior quality or an activity which the trademark owner would prefer not to be associated with.

2.2 Trademarks (unregistered)

If a company cannot rely on a registered trademark, it might instead be able to bring a claim in passing off. This is a tort which is sometimes described as similar to the continental European concept of unfair competition, but it is far narrower in its application. In the English courts, successful passing off claims have been brought on the basis of goodwill in the names of a business or its products, and also in relation to the get-up (ie, the appearance and packaging) of a product.

A successful claimant will need to establish:

- **Goodwill:** this will be shown if a business has customers in the UK, and it can demonstrate that this goodwill is attached to a particular word, shape or other feature of its business.
- **Misrepresentation:** typically, the misrepresentation will be that the defendant has implied, by using the same or similar get-up in which the claimant has goodwill, that the defendant's goods or services are those of or somehow connected to the claimant.
- **Damage:** finally, the claimant must show that it has or will suffer damage as a result of the defendant's misrepresentation.

Recent judgments demonstrate that, for the misrepresentation to be actionable, consumers must encounter the defendant's product and assume that it is from, or somehow connected to, the claimant. The English courts have generally been reluctant to find passing off, even where a claimant has been able to show that the defendant's product has been designed to look very much like the claimant's or even to 'wink to' the claimant's product. In *Moroccan Oil v Aldi*,[8] for example, the court refused to find passing off in respect of the two products, largely on the basis that a consumer encountering the defendant's

"In the UK, the process for obtaining a registered design right is short and relatively inexpensive."

product in an Aldi store would be very much aware that the product was not the claimant's given the presence of a different word trademark, the different price points of the competing products and also the propensity for own brand 'lookalike' products to be available in stores such as Aldi.

2.3 Designs (registered and unregistered)

In the UK, as in many other jurisdictions, there are registered and unregistered rights which provide for the protection of designs.

In the UK, a design can be registered for the appearance or physical shape of all or part of a product, provided that it:

- is **'new'**: meaning no identical or very similar design has been disclosed; and
- has **'individual character'**: meaning that the registered design must give a different 'overall impression' from previous designs which have been disclosed.

A design registration can subsist for 25 years. It provides the owner with a monopoly which can be enforced against any article which is made which does not create a different 'overall impression' from the registered design. There is no need for the owner to show that the defendant actually copied his design. This, as well as the term of protection, makes the registered design a much more valuable right than unregistered design rights.

In the UK, the process for obtaining a registered design right is short and relatively inexpensive. In part, this is because there is no thorough examination process undertaken before registration is granted. As a result, there may be a number of registered designs which would not stand up well to the scrutiny of an invalidity challenge.

Registered designs are used across the energy sector. Typically, they are used to protect the particular shape of all or part of a product which is used in the creation of energy or the dispensing of fuel products. For example, registered designs can be found on the UK register which protect the shape of an electric vehicle (EV) charging point, such as Shell's UK Registered Design No 6139797.

In addition to the registered regime described above, the design of a product can also give rise to unregistered design rights. These arise automatically and do not need to be registered.

In the UK, there are two regimes:

- The shape and configuration of a three-dimensional (3D) object

are protected by 'design right', which lasts for the shorter of 10 years from the sale of a product or 15 years from its creation.
- The appearance of a product (including its shape, colours, texture, material and ornamentation) can be protected as a 'supplementary unregistered design right'. This right was introduced following Brexit, and is designed to compensate for the loss of, and mimic, the unregistered Community design right which is available within the EU.

In each case, the owner of the right must prove not only that the defendant has made an article which shares the features of his design, but also that this similarity is the result of copying.

2.4 Copyright

Copyright arises automatically in the UK, upon the creation of an 'original' work. The UK legislation provides for the protection of original works in particular categories, such as literary, artistic and musical works.

Historically, copyright was considered to be appropriate almost exclusively for artistic creations. The UK, for example, has historically required 3D objects to have some aesthetic appeal and to be crafted by a skilled craftsman, in order to benefit from copyright protection as artistic works.

In contrast, purely functional shapes would potentially qualify for protection as design rights, with a much shorter lifespan than the protection afforded by copyright. This firm line dividing copyright and designs has become more blurred in recent years, particularly following decisions of the Court of Justice of the European Union (CJEU) in cases such as *Cofemel*,[9] in which the court ruled that EU member states could not require "aesthetic effect" as a condition for copyright protection. The only requirements were that a work was original (in the sense that it reflects an author's free and creative choices) and the subject matter must be identifiable with sufficient precision and originality. The subsequent decision of the CJEU in the *Brompton Bicycle*[10] case highlighted that everyday objects such as a folding bike could, theoretically, benefit from copyright protection even if the shape is, at least in part, necessary to obtain a technical effect.

In light of these decisions, there is the potential for a much wider range of works to be protected by copyright than has historically been the case. It is, therefore, possible that copyright will become as relevant to those in the energy sector as it is in the more obviously creative industries.

"The UK has historically required 3D objects to have some aesthetic appeal and to be crafted by a skilled craftsman, in order to benefit from copyright protection as artistic works."

3. Enforcement issues: jurisdiction, remedies and online enforcement

Securing one of the IP rights discussed above is, of course, only the first aspect of the process by which a brand can be protected. In this section, we briefly look at some of the key issues which arise in the enforcement of these IP rights.

3.1 Jurisdiction

All of the rights discussed in this chapter are territorial in nature and, therefore, only provide the owner with rights to prevent activity in the jurisdiction in which the right subsists.

Stopping infringing activities in multiple territories is, therefore, likely to require proceedings in multiple territories. Within the EU, actions for the infringement of EU Trademarks and Community Design Rights can be brought in one member state with remedies granted across the whole of the EU. The UK is no longer part of this system, following Brexit, and so separate proceedings will need to be commenced in the UK and an EU member state.

3.2 Remedies

Certain IP infringements amount to criminal offences, and criminal proceedings may be brought against those engaged in counterfeiting (particular forms of trademark infringement) and piracy (particular forms of copyright infringement), which can be a useful part of an energy company's armoury to protect its brands. In the UK, those convicted of criminal offences relating to counterfeiting can face both fines and prison sentences of up to 10 years.

In most cases which do not involve counterfeiting, claims will be brought in the civil courts by the holder of the IP right. A number of remedies are available to successful claimants in proceedings for the infringement of each of the IP rights discussed in this chapter.

The key goal for the majority of claimants in civil proceedings is an injunction to stop the defendant's infringing activity. A preliminary injunction, awarded pending trial, is also available in many jurisdictions in certain circumstances.

Successful claimants are typically entitled to recover financial compensation. In the UK, this is in the form of either damages or an account of the defendant's profits. The claimant can elect between the two after any trial on liability, on the basis of information provided to the claimant. In addition, successful claimants can also be awarded

"The key goal for the majority of claimants in civil proceedings is an injunction to stop the defendant's infringing activity."

either the delivery up or destruction of infringing goods, and an order that the defendant takes steps to publicise the judgment against it.

3.3 Online enforcement issues

A large number of brands disputes now take place in an online context. It is not possible to cover all aspects of such disputes in this chapter. Next, we discuss some of the key topics.

(a) Online marketplaces and social media platforms

Goods have been available for sale on online marketplaces since the very early days of the internet, with eBay, Amazon and Alibaba now some of the most popular. In recent years, social media platforms have also entered this space, with Facebook Marketplace and Instagram now the platforms of choice on which many brands sell or advertise their products.

Goods which infringe IP rights are also frequently offered for sale on these platforms. Enforcement action to prevent such sales can be taken in the usual way, by commencing court proceedings against the actual seller of the infringing goods. Online sales often raises other issues which can make the enforcement of IP rights more difficult.

First, it can often be difficult to identify, contact and locate the online sellers of infringing goods.

Secondly, and related to the first problem, questions arise as to the liability of the intermediaries whose platforms are used to advertise and sell infringing goods. This is a highly complex issue. The position will depend on a wide variety of factors, including: (1) the marketplace's precise role; (2) which particular IP rights are being infringed; and (3) the national laws regarding joint liability (which are not harmonised – even across the EU).

As a general rule, the infringement of a trademark is much harder to pin on an intermediary than the infringement of copyright because the intermediary is very unlikely to be 'using' the trademark even if their platform is being used to sell counterfeit goods.[11]

Despite these issues, it is worth bearing in mind that many intermediaries have established their own complaints and reporting procedures, which can be used to file notices of suspected IP infringements. The exact process varies by platform. In most circumstances, this process will provide rights owners with a much quicker, cheaper and more effective mechanism for the enforcement of their rights.

(b) Competitor keyword bidding

Another common online dispute is the use by one party (A) of the trademark of another party (B) as a keyword on advertising platforms such as Google AdWords.

This can result in Party A's advert being shown in response to a user searching for the trademark of Party B. Party B is then faced with a choice between: (1) not appearing (prominently, or at all) in the paid-for search results; or (2) paying more, to outbid their competitor, in order to appear.

This issue has been litigated in a number of cases and reached the CJEU. In short, the courts have taken the view that it is lawful to do this provided that the resulting advertisement enables an average internet user to ascertain whether the goods being advertised originate from the trademark owner or from a third party. Competitor keyword bidding is, therefore, now a common practice.

(c) Domain name disputes

Domain names have also been an area in which brands have been fiercely protective of their trademark rights.

There is a huge number of domains within the domain name system. In recent years, the generic top-level domains (such as .com and .org) and country code top-level domains (such as .co.uk) have been joined by newcomers such as .london.

The system has led, inevitably, to disputes between parties as to who is entitled to control domain names which contain a word protected by a trademark. Sometimes, such disputes arise where the same trademark is owned by two different parties in different territories, and both wish to control the domain name. Other disputes are the result of cybersquatting or the creation of fan sites or criticism sites.

Domain name disputes can typically be resolved reasonably quickly and cost-effectively. This is largely due to the existence of various dispute resolution services which have been established. The relevant dispute resolution service will depend on the domain. For example, the World Intellectual Property Organization (WIPO) administers complaints under its Uniform Domain Name Dispute Resolution Policy (UDRP) for disputes relating to .com. Nominet is the relevant organisation for disputes relating to .co.uk domains.

The precise requirements vary depending on the policy which is applied but, by way of illustration, a complaint made under WIPO's UDRP policy will need to show that:

"Domain name disputes can typically be resolved reasonably quickly and cost-effectively. This is largely due to the existence of various dispute resolution services which have been established. The relevant dispute resolution service will depend on the domain."

- the domain name complained of is either identical or confusingly similar to a trademark in which the complainant has rights;
- the registrant of the domain has no rights or legitimate interests in respect of the domain name; and
- the domain name was registered and is being used in bad faith.

Companies in the oil and gas industry have not always had success in taking action against criticism sites. Such sites are often defended on the basis that they make legitimate and non-commercial use of a trademark within a domain and do not mislead consumers or tarnish the trademark at issue. By way of example, in 2014, the Brazilian company Petroleo Brasileiro SA, owner of the well-known PETROBAS mark, was unsuccessful in its domain name complaint against the domain name www.maracutaiasnapetrobras.com (which roughly translates as 'dirty tricks at Petrobas'). The website contained allegations of corruption and criticism of the Brazilian government, which is a major shareholder in the company. Despite the registrant of the domain name not responding to the complaint, WIPO's Panel found that the use of the PETROBAS trademark in the domain was acceptable, on the basis that consumers would not be misled, and that the registrant had a legitimate interest in using the website to express its criticisms of the company and the Brazilian government.

4. Advertising disputes

Litigation can be costly, time-consuming and the results uncertain. Certain disputes with competitors can be resolved by bodies responsible for regulating advertisements, without the need for litigation.

In the UK, for example, the Advertising Standards Authority (ASA) is the independent advertising regulator. It responds to complaints raised by consumers as well as by competitors about claims made in advertising.

A large part of the ASA's role is to resolve complaints about adverts which are misleading, harmful and offensive. The ASA has limited enforcement powers, but it does publish adjudications and advertisers who are found to have breached the UK's advertising codes are informed that they must not run the same advert again.

The ASA is a particularly useful forum for complaints in the energy sector because:

- It takes a robust approach to claims about the environmental impact of products. Claims that a product is 'green', or 'greener' than an alternative, require a high level of substantiation and environmental claims must be made based on the full life cycle of the advertised product (unless the advert states otherwise).
- It will interrogate and make adjudications on the acceptability of comparative adverts, including those which use a competitor's trademark in order to make claims about the respective performance and capabilities of two products. The ASA assesses ads on similar criteria to those set out in the Comparative Advertising Directive.[12] This means that comparative adverts must objectively compare material, relevant, verifiable and representative features of products and must not cause confusion or denigrate the competitor's brand.

Resolving disputes through the ASA is typically a much faster and more cost-effective route than litigation.

5. Conclusion

Brand protection and the enforcement of rights is arguably more important now than it ever has been, as energy companies navigate the transition to renewable energy sources and consumers become even more aware of the long-term consequences of their energy consumption and the actions which brands are taking to address concerns about the health of the planet.

Energy companies looking to leverage their brands, therefore, need to consider the wide variety of IP rights which are available to them and the many avenues for enforcing those rights which we have touched on here.

If they do, and they manage to position themselves appropriately going forward, then it will be no surprise to see an energy company back in Forbes' Top 100 list in the not-too-distant future.

Notes

1 BP press release, "From International Oil Company to Integrated Energy Company: BP Sets Out Strategy for Decade of Delivery Towards Net Zero Ambition" (4 August 2020), www.bp.com/en/global/corporate/news-and-insights/press-releases/from-international-oil-company-to-integrated-energy-company-bp-sets-out-strategy-for-decade-of-delivery-towards-net-zero-ambition.html.
2 *Starbucks (HK) Ltd v British Sky Broadcasting Group Plc* [2012] EWHC 3074 (Ch) at [117].
3 UK00903349347.
4 *Société Des Produits Nestlé SA v Cadbury UK Ltd* [2013] EWCA Civ 1174 at [5] (emphasis added).
5 *BP Amoco plc v John Kelly Ltd* [2002] FSR 5.
6 *Och Ziff v OCH Capital* [2010] EWHC 2599 (Ch).
7 *Interflora Inc v Marks and Spencer plc* [2015] ETMR 5 (CA).
8 *Moroccanoil Israel Ltd v Aldi Stores Ltd* [2014] EWHC 1686 (IPEC).
9 *Cofemel – Sociedade de Vestuário SA v G-Star Raw CV* (C-683/17).
10 *Brompton Bicycle Ltd v Chedech/Get2Get* (C-833/18).
11 *L'Oreal SA v eBay International AG* (C-324/09).
12 Directive 2006/114/EC of the European Parliament and of the Council of 12 December 2006 concerning misleading and comparative advertising, https://eur-lex.europa.eu/legal-content/EN/TXT/?uri=celex%3A32006L0114.

About the authors

Charles T Collins-Chase
Partner, Finnegan LLP
charles.collins-chase@finnegan.com

Charles T Collins-Chase focuses on district court patent litigation and appeals before the US Court of Appeals for the Federal Circuit, where he served as a clerk. He uses his chemical engineering background to help clients protect innovations across the energy sector. In addition to his work in traditional oil and gas, Charles has also handled numerous matters involving renewable diesel fuel, solar installations, pollution control systems and bio-based polymers. Charles has extensive experience at the Federal Circuit, where he has argued cases and assisted clients in dozens of appeals from district courts and the Patent Trial and Appeal Board (PTAB). He has particular experience in appeals involving patent eligibility under 35 USC §101 and he was a member of the team representing the petitioners in *Bilski v Kappos* before the US Supreme Court.

Sean Ibbetson
Senior associate, Bristows LLP
Sean.Ibbetson@bristows.com

Sean Ibbetson is a senior associate in the brands, designs and copyright team at Bristows. He specialises in soft IP disputes and his recent litigation experience includes acting for: Vectura in passing off proceedings brought by GlaxoSmithKline; Fidelis in trademark infringement proceedings brought by Fidelity; Blizzard in liability proceedings and a subsequent account of profits for the sale of unauthorised 'cheats' and 'bots' for Blizzard's online games; luxury brands in disputes relating to the manufacture and sale of infringing items of jewellery; and Thomas Pink in High Court trademark infringement proceedings against Victoria's Secret.

Sean also advises brands and publishers on compliance with

advertising regulations, disputes with competitors and investigations by the UK's advertising regulator, the Advertising Standards Authority.

Kathryn R Judson
Associate, Finnegan LLP
kathryn.judson@finnegan.com

Kathryn R Judson is an associate in Finnegan Henderson's Atlanta, GA office, with experience in design patents, trademarks and patent litigation. Kathryn has an environmental science degree, as well as a law degree, and she has previous experience working on energy-related projects during her undergraduate studies.

Kathryn's work experience focuses primarily on pharmaceutical products, but she also has experience in renewable energy technologies.

Eoin Langford
Head of legal, BNRG Renewables Ltd
elangford@bnrg.ie

Eoin Langford is head of legal at the Irish solar development company, BNRG Renewables Ltd

Eoin holds a degree in law and a masters in European Integration and has specialised in Energy and Renewables projects and regulatory matters for nearly 20 years while based primarily in Dublin.

He has held senior in-house legal roles in companies such as EirGrid, OpenHydro and BNRG advising on a variety of legal topics, with a particular focus on project development, EPC contracting and project financing.

Jon Moorhouse
Partner, Keystone Law
jon.moorhouse@keystonelaw.co.uk

Jon Moorhouse is an intellectual property and commercial law partner at Keystone Law. He has over 20 years' international experience advising businesses of all sizes on a wide range of IP and commercial contractual matters, helping his clients to protect and commercialise their technology and to support this via IP strategies and IP governance and compliance programmes.

Jon has spent many years in-house with global corporations and has a keen focus on the energy sector having advised Shell for over 10 years as one of their senior lawyers, providing legal support to a range of projects, from large joint ventures to advising on spin-outs and investments in third-party 'new energies' start-ups and scale-ups via its strategic venture capital arm, Shell Ventures.

Maeve O'Flynn
Partner, Finnegan Europe LLP
maeve.oflynn@finnegan.com

Maeve O'Flynn is a European and UK patent attorney and is a partner at Finnegan Europe LLP. Maeve has more than a decade of in-house experience, having worked at some of the world's largest multinational corporations in the oil and chemical industries. She has worked for a range of clients, from start-ups to multinationals, covering diverse technologies such as cosmetics, sustainable chemistry and catalysis. Maeve has helped clients develop commercially relevant intellectual property strategies. This includes: developing and managing global patent portfolios; provisioning advice regarding trade secrets and defensive publications; and negotiating collaboration and licensing agreements.

Maeve has extensive experience preparing and prosecuting patent applications, from the initial invention harvesting sessions through to achieving allowance. She works with clients to assess and value their patent portfolios, and to develop filing strategies that support their commercial aims. She also represents clients at oral proceedings before the European Patent Office, representing both patentee and opponent.

Robert Pocknell
Consultant solicitor, Keystone Law
robert.pocknell@keystonelaw.co.uk

Robert Pocknell is a consultant solicitor with Keystone Law and has specialised in intellectual property matters for more than 30 years. Robert has advised multinationals and SMEs on IP strategies and has worked both in-house and in private practice.

Robert was the founding chairman of the Fair Standards Alliance, a Brussels-based organisation advocating for fairer and more reasonable licensing practices for standard essential patents. The alliance is the leading industry voice for standard essential patents, and has grown to more than 50 members, across, up and down the telecoms and IoT supply chains.

Robert has been listed as a Top 300 World IP Strategist by IAM Media for several years.

Paul Townsend
Associate, Finnegan LLP
paul.townsend@finnegan.com

Paul Townsend is an associate in Finnegan Henderson's Washington DC office, with experience in both patent prosecution and litigation. Paul has a chemical engineering degree, as well as a law degree, and he has previous engineering experience in the energy industry.

Paul's work experience extends across a broad range of subjects, including energy-related technologies, polymers, coatings, catalysts, speciality chemicals and pharmaceutical products, with a particular interest in technologies relating to the energy industries.

About Globe Law and Business

Globe Law and Business was established in 2005. From the very beginning, we set out to create law books which are sufficiently high level to be of real use to the experienced professional, yet still accessible and easy to navigate. Most of our authors are drawn from Magic Circle and other top commercial firms, both in the UK and internationally.

Our titles are carefully produced, with the utmost attention paid to editorial, design and production processes. We hope this results in high-quality publications that are easy to read, and a pleasure to own. Our titles are also available as ebooks, which are compatible with most desktop, laptop and tablet devices. In 2018 we expanded our portfolio to include journals and Special Reports, available both digitally and in hard copy format, and produced to the same high standards as our books.

In the spring of 2021, we were very pleased to announce the start of a new chapter for Globe Law and Business following the acquisition of law books under the imprint Ark Publishing. We are very much looking forward to working with our Ark authors, many of whom are well known to us, to further developing the law firm management list, and to welcoming our new Ark customers.

We'd very much like to hear from you with your thoughts and ideas for improving what we offer. Please do feel free to email me at sian@globelawandbusiness.com with your views.

Sian O'Neill
Managing director
Globe Law and Business
www.globelawandbusiness.com